Professionals of Hope
The Selected Writings of
Subcomandante Marcos

Afterword by Gabriela Jauregui

The Song Cave

Published by The Song Cave
www.the-song-cave.com
2017

Design and layout by Mary Austin Speaker

ISBN: 978-0-9967786-5-7

Library of Congress Control Number: 2017945866

FIRST EDITION

TABLE OF CONTENTS

Professionals of Hope

THERE WILL BE A STORM
OCTOBER 8, 1994

To the national magazine Proceso
To the national newspaper La Jornada
To the national newspaper El Financiero
To the local newspaper in San Cristobal de las Casas Tiempo

Sirs:

I don't know why they say that Mexico has changed, that a new democratic era has begun for the country. I don't know about there, but here everything is the same. The PRI perjures itself and swears (after a disgraceful fraud) that it won fairly. Ranchers and businessmen join in, saying that they "respect the will of the people"—in other words, they are saying that they only respect their own will. The Catholic Church is an accomplice (to the fraud). The indigenous peasants know that the PRI didn't win fairly. They aren't going to endure another PRI governor. They know that a traitor to his own blood can't be allowed to govern.

Little by little, the Chiapanec world is beginning to divide. The wind from above assumes its old forms of arrogance and haughtiness. The police and the Federal Army close ranks around money and corruption. The wind from below once again travels the ravines and valleys; it is beginning to blow strongly. There will be a storm...

We are in the same situation that existed in December of 1993; the country is living in a euphoria of high economic indicators, political stability, promises of better times for ordinary citizens, and promises of continued stability for powerful citizens. In Chiapas there is a PRI government that is said to have "popular support." The country is calm. Everyone is calm... and then, the first hour of January First... Enough already! No? OK. I wish you good health and hope you have a little understanding for what's coming.

From the mountains of Southeastern Mexico,
Subcomandante Insurgente Marcos.

P.S. Ana Maria tells me that "the water is rising in the mountain streams." I look worriedly at the greyness that is stretched across the horizon. She adds, "If it doesn't stop raining, those streams are going to run as they never have before." She goes off to check the guards. "As they never have before," I mutter. I light my pipe. Old Man Antonio approaches me and asks for a light for his cigarette. I shelter the lighter's flame with my hands. I can just see, in that brief light, that Antonio is crying. Ana Maria returns. She comes to attention and reports. Then she asks, "The troops are ready. What are we going to do?" I look once again at the greyness that is spreading across the sky and dominating the night. I answer her with a sigh, "We wait. We wait..."

P.P.S. One of the mysteries of Ezeelen is uncovered. A lively and violent wind, sweet and bitter, blows a paper to the feet of an indigenous peasant. On the paper one can read:

Declaration of Principles of the EZLN:
A certain dose of tenderness is necessary in order to walk when there is so much against you, to wake up when you're so exhausted. A certain dose of tenderness is necessary in order to see, in this darkness, a small ray of light in order to make order from shame and obligations. A certain dose of tenderness is necessary in order to get rid of all of the sons of bitches that exist. But sometimes a certain dose of tenderness is not enough and it's necessary to add...a certain dose of bullets.

MARCOS IN THE LIBRARY
JANUARY 18, 1995

To the weekly magazine Proceso
To the national newspaper EL Financiero
To the national newspaper La Jornada
To the local newspaper of SCLC Tiempo

Sirs:

Here go some communiqués which indicate a change of direction in the winds. You are threatening us with unemployment again. I hope this time it's serious. They tell me that Mr. Robledo Rincon (fraudulently elected PRI Governor of Chiapas) is huddled with his armed guards, self-named "state public security police," somewhere in the governor's palace. Even though those who oppose the popular will are limited to four neighborhoods of the old capital of Chiapas, Tuxtla Gutierrez, a dignified exit can be offered them. They should just explain where the money came from to arm the white guards who assassinate indigenous people in the Chiapanec countryside. Perhaps it is the money from the "peace agreements" of San Cristobal that never reached the poor of this state in the Mexican Southeast (we're still called "Mexico"? No?).

OK. *Salud,* and a peace of hope to foretell tomorrow.

From the mountains of the Mexican Southeast,
Subcomandante Insurgente Marcos.

P.S. He remembers a previous morning and a cold interior. One night of tanks, planes, and helicopters, I was in the library of Aguascalientes. Alone, surrounded by books and a cold rain which forced the use of the ski mask—not to hide from anyone's eyes, but to hide from the cold. I sat in one of the few chairs which was still intact, and contemplated the abandonment of the place. That dawn was, like others, empty of people. The Library began its complicated ceremony of exposition. The heavy bookcases began a movement much like a disorganized dance. The books changed places, and in the motion one of them fell and exposed an undamaged page. I did not pick it up, but moved between dancing shelves in order to get close enough to read it...

"The Library exists *ab aeterno*. No reasonable mind can doubt this truth, whose immediate corollary is the future eternity of the world. Man, the imperfect librarian, may be the work of chance or of malevolent demiurges; the universe, with its elegant endowment of shelves, of enigmatic volumes, of indefatigable ladders for the voyager, and of privies for the seated librarian, can only be the work of a god...The impious assert that absurdities are the norm in the Library and that anything reasonable (even humble and pure coherence) is almost a miraculous exception... *The Library is limitless and periodic.* If an eternal voyager were to traverse it in any direction, he would find, after many centuries, that the same volumes would be repeated in the same disorder (which, repeated, would constitute an order: Order itself). My solitude rejoices in this elegant hope.*

*Leticia Alvarez de Toledo has observed that the vast Library is useless. Strictly speaking, *one single volume* should suffice: a single volume of ordinary format, printed in nine or ten point type, and consisting of an infinite number of infinitely thin pages (...) The silky vade mecum would scarcely be handy: each apparent leaf would divide into other analogous leaves. The inconceivable central leaf would have no reverse."

—Jorge Luis Borges, *The Library of Babel*

"My solitude rejoices in this elegant hope," I repeat as I slip away from the library. Aguascalientes is deserted. I am tempted to say "abandoned," when a fox runs across towards the kitchen. The Library continues its metamorphosis. Noises, creaks, and imaginary laments escape through doors and windows. Did I say doors? It has two holes which are impossible to define. There is that which allows one to enter, which some say is an exit, others argue that the library breathes through them, some suspect that they are for gulping people, animals, and hopes. The Library of Aguascalientes is the beginning and the end of the spiral, and it does not have a defined entrance nor exit. I mean to say that in the gigantic spiral which Tacho described in order to explain the architectural origin of Aguascalientes, the Library is in the beginning and the end. The safe-house which "kept the greatest secrets of the organization," is at the other end, the beginning of the whirl. I run my eyes over the gigantic spiral in which the construction is aligned, and I imagine that from a satellite in space one can appreciate the spiral which "calls from the jungle." My gaze runs from the safe-house to the Library, which now gives out a phosphorescent blue and a continuous, hoarse noise. The Library tells what can be thought, and by day, is inhabited by children. They don't come here because of the books. They say, according to what Eva told me, that there are multi-colored balloons here. Apparently no one finds them, because the children end up painting colorful pictures. Lately, helicopters and planes are abundant, not just in the skies above Aguascalientes, but also in the flat pictures of the children. The purples, reds, and greens are much too abundant in the pictures for my liking. Yellow seems to limit itself to the sun which, these days, is covered by the grey of the sky. At night, the Library shelters and agitates transgressors of the law and professionals of violence (like the one who writes this). They gaze at the shelves filled with books looking for something that is missing, and which they're sure was once there. The Library was the only thing, in all Aguascalientes, considered the property of the Democratic National Convention, and it sometimes has books. The caravaneers made efforts to give it electricity, bookshelves, books, tables, chairs, and an old computer which has the virtue of having never being used. The rest of Aguascalientes has remained abandoned since that 9th day of August, 1994. Now the Library remains silent, the phosphorescence is concentrated in one point, in its center, and it turns emerald green. I move carefully to one of the windows. The green light was blinding and it took some time to get used to looking at. In it I saw, all of a sudden, the blue sails of Aguascalientes caught in a favorable wind. I turned toward the command post but it remained empty. The sea thrust its waves against the keel and the creaking of the chains of the anchor could be heard above the wind. I climbed in starboard and took the rudder in order to free it from the labyrinth of the spiral. Was it leaving or arriving? The emerald of the library went out.

P.S. THAT HE REPEATS WHAT WAS TOLD TO HIM FROM THE LANDS OF ZAPATA: *Cruelty in Uaymil-Chetumal...*

Ten years after Alonso Davila was flung out from Villa Real de Chetumal, the rash Francisco de Montejo again considered the conquest of the province of Uaymil-Chetumal (1543-1545). He commissioned Gaspar Pacheco, his son Melchor, and 30 soldiers for this action. Thus they began the desolate war of Uaymil-Chetumal. A report of the era stated: "Mayan men and women, in equal measure, were killed with clubs, or thrown into the lakes with weights tied on their feet so that they would drown. Savage dogs used in the war tore them to pieces, these defenseless Indians. The Spanish considered them animals, and they dragged and beat them like animals. It is said that the Pachecos cut the hands, the ears, and the noses off of many Indians."

As you can see, the bad government began many years ago and its methods are somewhat passé...

I, meanwhile, look worriedly at my "prominent nose," now red and cold because of what they write about "cutting their noses."

Greetings to the pipe of Popocatepetl, and always remember that...

"In Popocatepetl aic ixpolihuiz, in mexicayotl aic ixpolihuiz, Zapata nemi iyihtic tepetl, iyihtic macehuiltin."

(Look: it is Nahuatl). OK once again.

The Supmarine from the high seas.

THE ZAPATISTAS HIKE UP THE PRICE OF INDIGENOUS MEXICAN BLOOD

FEBRUARY 9, 1995

To the national weekly Proceso
To the national newspaper El Financiero
To the national newspaper La Jornada
To the local paper of San Cristobal de Las Casas Tiempo

Gentlemen:

Here goes a communiqué...the last one, as we see the events. The Zapatistas hike up the price of Indigenous Mexican blood. Yesterday it was worth less than a backyard bird. Today its death is the condition of the loan of greatest infamy in the world's history. The price of Zapatista heads is the only price that maintains a high value in the ups and downs of financial speculation. Mr. Zedillo is beginning to repay the loan. His message is clear. Either you speak with submission and kneel down in front of the supreme government, or with support of my accomplices in the Congress, I will annihilate you. Now he is making up proof that we do not want dialogue? What is his objective? To pay the loan. Somebody should tell this man who the Zapatistas are. He seems not to have ever talked to people with dignity. He is inexperienced in relating to human beings. He knows how to deal with figures, macroeconomic plans, a lying media, and submissive opponents, but not with human beings. We will see if he learns before he breaks everything.

The first and most enthusiastic applause to the ultimatum in Queretaro, and to the "spectacular coup" of February 9, comes from the great landowners and great merchants of the Southeast. They know that their private armies do not have the guts to confront the Zapatistas. Now they hope that the federal army will do the job that they used to do themselves without so much media attention: massive assassinations.

The supreme government threatens us...The Zapatistas.

The Zapatistas, and not the ones who are mainly responsible for the present and future misery of millions of Mexicans, for unemployment, the low level of incomes, for the lost confidence in the supreme government and its "institutions."

The Zapatistas, and not those who, with funds from the Mexican people, travel to sell economic fallacies in other countries.

The Zapatistas, and not the upper hierarchy of the church, who while we eat beans, chiles, and tortillas, sit at great banquets, and ask about the "dark" financing of the ezzee-el-aen (ezetaelene), EZLN.

The Zapatistas, and not Hank Gonzalez, whom the U.S. State Department is tracking down for the laundering of dollars and his ties to narco drug trafficking. What Mexican justice should be doing, is being done by the U.S.

The Zapatistas, and not those who knew of the December devaluation, and celebrated with champagne the floating of the peso (an elegant way of describing a sudden collapse).

The Zapatistas, and not those surrounding the great lie of the Salinista boom, who embroider the complicated net of theoretic caravans and "brilliant" and "objective" addendum analysis to sing praises to the macro-lie.

The Zapatistas, and not those in Chiapas, Tabasco, Veracruz, Tlaxcala, San Luis Potosi, Guanajuato, Jalisco, who perpetrated, and now prepare, a greater economic fraud, the fraud of the hopes for the peaceful transition to democracy.

The Zapatistas, and not those who raped the Tzetzal Indigenous women in Altamirano.

The Zapatistas, and not those who executed, with a *coup de grace*, the insurgent combatants detained in the market of Ocosingo.

The Zapatistas, and not those who, with elegant clarification said that bombs were not used, dropped "rockets" on civilian populations in San Cristobal, Los Altos, and the jungle.

The Zapatistas, and not those who use hunting dogs to persecute civilians.

The Zapatistas, and not those who appraised indigenous blood in the stock exchange of Chiapas to be worth less than the price of a chicken.

The Zapatistas, and not those who pocketed the money of the "peace agreements" in San Cristobal.

The Zapatistas, and not those who, from the impunity of their fraudulent curule (Senate seat), violated and continue to violate the Constitution.

The Zapatistas, and not those responsible for the crime, who now retain the power over the energy wealth of Mexico.

The Zapatistas, and not those who were active or passive accomplices of the greatest crime since Porfirio Diaz: Salinismo.

The Zapatistas, and not those who live the "insecurity" of a salary of thousands of pesos a month, in exchange for the "tiring" exercise of raising a finger to approve the sale of the homeland yesterday, and today the extermination of the indigenous people of the Southeast.

The Zapatistas, and not the political arm of organized crime and narco-drug trafficking, which in addition dares to boast as a most supreme insult, the colors of the national flag in its seal.

The Zapatistas, and not the handful of U.S. capitalists who already paid, in advance, for the purchase of our wealth, underground.

The Zapatistas, and not those who, from the pulpit of mass media, lied, lie, and will lie to the nation.

The Zapatistas, and not those who in January, 1995, introduced themselves in Switzerland, to the IMF, saying, "President Salinas has instructed me...Excuse me, I mean President Zedillo..."

The Zapatistas, and not those who, from the IDB, with a foreign race and vocation, lead the destiny of our country.

The Zapatistas, and not the white guards.

The Zapatistas, the men and women who rose up in arms so as not to live on their knees anymore, and not those who for centuries have kept us down in ignorance, misery, death, and hopelessness.

The Zapatistas, the ones who decided to give their life as guarantee that they never again will talk under anyone's threats.

The Zapatistas, the littlest ones, always forgotten—the flesh destined yesterday to death by diarrhea, malnutrition, forgotten in the coffee fields, in the landowners' fields, the streets, the mountain.

The Zapatistas, the littlest ones, always forgotten—the flesh destined tomorrow to serve as exercise polygon for the modern armament of an army, which instead of defending national sovereignty, point their weapons against the traitors of the homeland, point them to their siblings in blood, soil, and history.

The Zapatistas, the millionaires of undelivered promises, the ones who cover their faces, so that their brothers and sisters in other lands can see them.

The Zapatistas, the ones of "for everybody everything, nothing for us."

The Zapatistas, the ones who teach the present rulers what they did not learn in their graduate studies abroad, and what is not in the textbooks of the ones who mis-educate the Mexican children: i.e. shame, dignity for human beings, and love for homeland and history.

The Zapatistas, the ones who, in the middle of a country of fritters, foreign goods, "great" macroeconomic achievements, fictitious first worlds, and despairs of change, drew up in the soil and sky of these lands, the six letters that had already been sold cheap in the international market: Mexico.

The Zapatistas, the men, women, children, and old people who (long before those who today usurp the Mexican will, were a dream even in the blood of their last generation) reside, live, and die in these lands. The ones who, together with other indigenous people, gave to this country the image of the eagle devouring a serpent as our national seal.

The Zapatistas, we, you, all the ones who are not themselves...

Anyway, whatever happens, thanks to everybody for everything. If we were to turn back the clock of history, we would not doubt for a second doing again what we have done. One time, one thousand times we would say again, "*Ya Basta*," "Enough."

OK, a salute and a strong, strong embrace (for the cold and so that we do not allow forgetfulness to reign again).

From the mountains of Southeast Mexico,
Subcomandante Insurgente Marcos.

P.S. Applauding furiously the new "success" of the government police: I heard that they discovered another Marcos, and he is very tampiqueño (from Tampico). It does not sound bad; the port is beautiful. I remember when I was working as a bouncer in a brothel in Ciudad Madero during the times in which La Quina did to the regional economy what Salinas did to the stock exchange: inject money to hide poverty. I left the port because humidity makes me sleepy, and seafood makes the sleepiness go away.

P.P.S. Not going away, in spite of the circumstances, it's narcissism: Well, and so, this new Subcomandante Marcos, is he handsome? It's because lately they have only thrown at me ugly ones, and it ruins all the correspondence from females.

P.P.S. Counting ammunition and time: I have 300 shots, so try to bring more than 299 soldiers and policemen to catch me (legend has it that I don't miss... Do you want to find out?). Why 299 if there are 300 bullets? Well, the last one is for "yours truly." It happens that one becomes fond of things like that, and a bullet seems the only consolation for a solitary chest.

OK again.

Salud, and ?

Would there be a little peace in her bosom for a memory?

The sup, retouching the ski-mask with macabre flirtation.

A YEAR OF ZAPATISTA GOVERNMENT
MARCH 17, 1995

To the men and women who, in different tongues and roads, believe in a more humane future, and are struggling to achieve it today:

Brothers and sisters:

There exists on this planet called "Earth" and in the continent called "America," a country whose shape appears to have had a big bite taken out of its west side, and which threw out an arm deep into the Pacific Ocean so that the hurricanes wouldn't blow it far away from its history. This country is known to both natives and foreigners by the name of "Mexico." Its history is a long battle between its desire to be itself and the foreign desires to have it exist under another flag. This country is ours.

Our blood is in the voices of our oldest grandparents; we walked this land when it was not yet known by this name. But later in this eternal struggle, between being and not being, between staying and leaving, between yesterday and tomorrow, our ancestors began to believe that this piece of land, water, sky, and dreams, the land that we had because it had been given as a gift from our earlier ancestors, would be called "Mexico." Then we became more, and the history of the name was complete. And we were called "Mexicans."

Later, history continued to deliver blows and pains. We were born between blood and gunpowder; between blood and gunpowder we were raised. Every so often, powerful people from other lands came to rob us of our tomorrow. For this reason, we fought yesterday. With different flags and different languages, the foreigner came to conquer us. He came and he went. We continued to be Mexicans, because we weren't happy with any other name, nor to walk under any other flag that does not have the eagle devouring a snake on a white background, with green and red on the edges.

We, the first inhabitants of these lands, the indigenous people, were left forgotten in a corner, while the rest began to grow and become stronger. We only had our history with which to defend ourselves, and we seized it in order not to die. Later, even this part of the history became a joke because a single country, the country of money, put itself in the middle of all of the flags. And they said "Globalization," and then we knew that this is what this absurd order was called, an order in which money is the only country, and the borders are erased, not out of brotherhood, but because of the impoverishment which fattens the powerful without nationality. The lie became the universal coin, and in our country, a dream based on the nightmare of the majority of wealth and prosperity was knitted for the few.

Corruption and falsehoods were the principal products that our Motherland exported to other countries. Being poor, dressed in the wealth of our scarcities, and because there were so many lies and they were so broad, we ended up thinking they were the truth. We prepared for the great international forums, and poverty was declared by the will of the government. And us? We became even more forgotten, and our history wasn't enough to keep us from dying, forgotten and humiliated. Because death does not hurt: what hurts is to be forgotten. We discovered then that we did not exist anymore, that those who govern had forgotten about us in their euphoria of statistics and rates of growth.

A country that forgets itself is a sad country, and a country that forgets its past cannot have a future. And so we took up arms and we went into the cities where we were considered animals. We went and we told the powerful, "We are here!" And to all of the country we shouted, "We are here!" And to all of the world we yelled, "We are here!" And they saw how things were, because in order for them to see us, we covered our faces; so that they would call us by name, we gave up our names; we bet the present to have a future; and to live...we died. And then the planes came, and the bombs and the bullets and the death, and we went back to our mountains, and even there death pursued us, and many people from many parts said, "Talk," and the powerful said, "Let's talk," and we said, "Okay, let's talk," and we talked and we told them what we wanted, and they did not understand very well, and we repeated that we wanted democracy, liberty, and justice, and they made a face like they didn't understand, and they reviewed their macroeconomic plans and all their neoliberal points, and they could not find these words anywhere, and "We don't understand," was all they said to us, and they offered us a prettier corner in the history museum, and death with an extended timeline, and a chain of gold in order to tie up our dignity. And, so that they would understand what we wanted, we began to create in our own lands what we wanted. We organized based on the agreement of the majority, and we demonstrated what it was like to live with democracy, with liberty, and with justice. This is what happened:

For a year the law of the Zapatistas governed the mountains of Southeastern Mexico, and you all were not there to know about it, nor can I tell it, but we are Zapatistas. In other words, those of us who do not have a face, name, or a past, and for the most part are indigenous people. But lately more brothers and sisters of other lands and races have participated. All of us are Mexicans. When we governed these lands we did the following:

When we governed, we lowered to zero the rate of alcoholism, and the women here became very fierce and they said that drink only served to make the men beat their women and children, and to act barbarically, and therefore they gave the order that no drink was allowed, and that we could not allow drinking to go on, and the people who received the most benefit were the children and women, and the ones most damaged were the businessmen and the government. And, with the support of some of those groups called "Non-Governmental Organizations," both from within the country and foreigners, health campaigns were carried out, and the hope for life for the civilian population was raised, even though the lack of trust in the government reduced the hope for our lives, the combatants. And the women began to see that the laws which were imposed on the men were fulfilled; and a third of our combatant force is made up of women, and they are very fierce, and they are armed; and so they "convinced" us to accept their laws and they also participate in the civilian and military direction of our struggle and we don't say anything; and besides, what are we going to say?

The destruction of trees also was prohibited, and laws were made to protect the forests, and the hunting of wild animals was prohibited, and the cultivation, consumption, and trafficking in drugs was prohibited, and these laws were upheld. The infant mortality rate went way down, and became very small, just like the children. And the Zapatista laws were applied uniformly, without regard for social position or income level. And we made all of the major decisions, or the "strategic" ones, of our struggle, by means of a method that they call the "referendum" and the "plebiscite." And we got rid of prostitution, and unemployment disappeared as well as begging. The children had sweets and toys. And we made many errors and had many failures. And we also accomplished what no other government in the world, regardless of its political affiliation, is capable of doing honestly, and that is to recognize its errors and to take steps to remedy them.

We were doing this, learning, when the tanks and the helicopters and planes and the many thousands of soldiers arrived, and they told us they were there to defend national sovereignty, and we told them that national sovereignty was being violated in the U.S.A., not in Chiapas, and that it cannot be defended by trampling the rebel dignity of the Chiapas indigenous communities. But they did not listen, because the noise of their war machines made them deaf and they came in the name of the government, and for the government, betrayal is the ladder by which one climbs to power. For us, loyalty is the egalitarian plane that we desire for everyone. And the legality of the government came mounted on bayonets, and our legality was based on consensus and reason. We wanted to convince, and the government wanted to conquer. We said that no law that needed to resort to arms in order to be fulfilled by a people could be called a law. It is arbitrary how many legalist wrappings it is covered with, he who orders the fulfillment of a law accompanied by the force of weapons, is a dictator. Even if he says that the majority elected him. So we were run out of our lands. With the war tanks came the law of the government, and the law of the Zapatistas left. Behind the war tanks of the government again came prostitution, drinking, theft, drugs, destruction, death, corruption, sickness, and poverty.

People from the government came, and said that they had now restored law in the Chiapas lands, and they came with bulletproof vests and with war tanks, and that they were there for only a few minutes, that they just had enough time to say their statements in front of the chickens and roosters and pigs and dogs and cows and horses and a cat that had gotten lost. And that's how the government did it. Maybe you all know this because it's true, that a lot of reporters saw this and publicized it. And this is the law that rules our lands now. This is how the government conducted the war for "legality" and for "national sovereignty" against the indigenous people of Chiapas. The government also waged war against the rest of the Mexicans, but instead of tanks and planes, they launched an economic program that is also going to kill them, just more slowly...

And now I remember that I am writing on March 17th, St. Patrick's Day, and when Mexico was fighting, in the last century, against the empire of the crooked stars and stripes, there was a group of soldiers of different nationalities who fought on the side of the Mexicans, and this group was called the "St. Patrick's Battalion," and for this reason the compañeros said to me: "Go on, take this opportunity to write to the brothers from other countries and thank them, because they stopped the war," but I believe that this is their way of distracting me so that they get to go dance, and so that I don't yell at them to stay in because the government planes are flying around here, and all these compañeros want to do is to dance, even with everything, and the war, they keep dancing and dancing the marimba. And so I am writing to you in the name of all of my compañeros and compañeras, because just as with the St. Patrick's Battalion, we now see clearly that there are foreigners who love Mexico more than some natives who are in the government, and tomorrow who will be in jail or in physical exile, because their heart now belongs to foreigners, because they love a flag which is not theirs, and another way of thinking which is not of their equals. We learned that there were marches and songs and movies and other things that were not war in Chiapas, which is the part of Mexico where we live and die. We learned that "NO TO WAR!" was yelled in Spain, France, Italy, Germany, Russia, England, Japan, Korea, Canada, the United States, Argentina, Uruguay, Chile, Venezuela, Brazil, and in other parts where it wasn't yelled, but it was thought. And so we saw that there are good people in many parts of the world, and that these people live closer to Mexico than those who live in "Los Piños," our house of government.

Our own laws made books, medicine, laughter, sweets, and toys flourish. Their law, the law of the powerful, came without any argument other than that of force, and it destroyed our libraries, clinics, and hospitals. It brought sadness to our people. We thought laws that destroy knowledge, health, and happiness would seem stupid to such big women and men, and that our laws are better, infinitely better than the law of these foreign men who say that they govern us.

And we want to say to you, to everyone, thank you. And that if we had a flower, we would give it to you, and since we don't have enough flowers for each man or woman, but there's enough so that each person can get and save a piece, and when they are old they can talk with their children and the young people of their country about how "I struggled for Mexico at the end of the 20th century, from over here I was there with them, and I know that they wanted what all human beings want, to not to be forgotten as human beings and for democracy, liberty, and justice to be known. I didn't know their faces, but I did know their hearts, and they were the same as ours." And when Mexico is free (which is not to say happy or perfect, but only free, or in other words, free to choose its own road and make its own mistakes and its successes) then a piece of you all, this heart at the top of our chests that, despite the political implications or precisely because of them, is a little tilted to the left, will also be Mexico; and these six letters will represent dignity. It occurs to me now that with this letter a paper flower could be made and could be put in the lapel or in one's hair, depending on the person, and you could go out dancing with this enchanting adornment. I'm going to go now because the surveillance plane is coming again, and I have to blow out the candle, but not the hope. This...nor death.

Goodbye...
Salud, and a promised flower: a green stem, with a white flower and red leaves. Don't worry about the snake in our flag; there next to it, flapping its wings, is an eagle. The eagle is in charge, as you will soon see...

From the mountains of Southeastern Mexico,
Subcomandante Insurgente Marcos.

THAT REASON ALWAYS WINS AND NEVER FORCE
MARCH 25, 1995

For the Civic Society
Aguascalientes, Chiapas, Mexico

Brothers and sisters:

Welcome to Zapatista territory, which is to say "territory in rebellion against evil government." That is how things are, even though these lands are filled with war. Even though they want to trample dignity with war tanks and even though they want to shut up reason with the noise of planes and helicopters.

We wanted to participate personally in this dialogue, but there are approximately 60,000 olive green reasons that prevent us from doing so. It doesn't matter; we hope that you accept this letter as the means by which our voice, our thinking, and our hearts can reach all of you, who, after detaining the government's war, came to our lands to reaffirm the search for civic and peaceful ways to resolve the problems that we, both nationals and foreigners, suffer from in this last part of the 20th century.

We hope that this will not be the last time that you visit us, and that many of you will be able to stay in the "Peace Camps" that are located in various villages in the state of Chiapas, and which have made it possible for our civilian brothers and sisters to return to their homes.

We hope, also, that on another occasion we can be present to receive you, as it is the custom to receive brothers and sisters: with flowers and the music of marimbas. We owe you those two things, in addition to everything else that we owe you.

In continuation, we present to you our proposal for a "Complementary Protocol" to be incorporated into the "Universal Social Convention" which will be approved by you. We are clear that our proposal is equivalent to all the others, that it is subject to discussion, and we will respect the decision that you make.

Complementary Protocol for the Universal Social Convention

We, human beings, here today in this place, demand:

1. That reason always wins and never force.

2. That the majority do what a majority does, imposing its will on the minority, without the minority disappearing or having its right to become the majority restricted.

3. That any man can give any woman any flower in any part of any world, and that this woman give thanks for the flower not with just any smile, but with the best and only one.

4. That the morning no longer be a great question or a disaster waiting to happen; that the morning be just that: the morning.

5. That the night not be a cave of fear; that the night be a bed of desire.

6. That sadness be surprised with a simple look of disdain; and that happiness and laughter be free and never lacking.

7. That for everyone there be, always, bread to illuminate the table, education to feed ignorance, health to surprise death, land to harvest a future, a roof to shelter hope, and work to make hands dignified.

8. That the words and hearts of men and women no longer be prisoners of jails, tombs, or threats.

9. That war be part of a long ago and foreign past, and that neither armies nor soldiers be necessary any longer.

10. That those who govern command by obeying. That those who do not fulfill this be exchanged for others.

11. That there always exists someone who is willing to struggle so that all that came before becomes not a demand, but a reality.

Respectfully,
From the mountains of Southeastern Mexico,
Subcomandante Insurgente Marcos.

LETTER TO EDUARDO GALEANO
MAY 11, 1995
MONTEVIDEO, URUGUAY

Mr. Galeano:

I'm writing to you because...because I feel like writing to you. Because Children's Day just ended, and it occurs to me that I might talk to you about what happens in a child's day in the middle of a secret war here in Mexico. I'm writing to you because I have no reason for doing so, which means that I can tell you things as they occur to me, without worrying that I stray from the purpose of this letter. I'm also writing to you because I have lost the book you gave me, because Destiny's sleight of hand has replaced it with another, because a passage in your book *Las Palabras Andantes (Walking Words)* keeps dancing around in my head. Because it asks:

> Do words know how to fall silent when they can't find the time or place for which they're called? And the mouth, does it know how to die?

And so I have sat down to smoke and think. It's dawn. For a pillow I have a rifle. (Okay, it's not really a rifle; it's a police carbine that until January 1994 was used to kill indigenous people. Now, it serves to protect them.) With my boots on and a pistol within easy reach, I think and smoke. Outside the ring of smoke and thoughts, May lies to herself and pretends she's June, and now a rainstorm's thunder and lightning have managed the seemingly impossible feat of silencing the crickets.

But I'm not thinking of the rain. No. I'm not trying to guess which of the lightning bolts that rip the fabric of the night spells death. No. I'm not worrying that the nylon trap is too small to cover my dwelling and that the side of my bed is getting soaked. (Ah! Because it just so happens that I made my bed out of boughs and poles fastened with vines. It is a desk, a storage space, and sometimes a bed. I can't get comfortable in the hammock, or rather I get too comfortable. I sleep very soundly, and deep sleep is a luxury that you can pay for very dearly around here. This bed of sticks is uncomfortable enough that a wink could be called sleep.)

No, I am not worried about the night, the rain, or the thunder. What worries me is that business of "Do words fall silent when they can't find the time or place for which they're called? And the mouth, does it know how to die?"

Ana María, an indigenous Tzotzil who is an infantry major in our army, sent me the book. Someone sent it to her, and she sent it to me, not knowing that I had lost your book, and that this one is replacing the lost one, which is almost the same but not quite; this one is full of little drawings in black ink. That's how books and words should be, I think, with little drawings that pop out of the head or the mouth or the hands, dancing on the page each time the book is opened, dancing in the heart each time the book is read. The book is the greatest gift man has given to himself. But let's get back to your book, the one I have now. I read it by the light of a little candle stub I found in my backpack. The wick gave up on the last passage on page 262 (A palindrome, no? A sign?). So, I remembered the Perón quote you relayed to me and my awkward response, and, later, the book you sent me. And now I am embarrassed to tell you that I abandoned the book in February's "lucky escape." Now I have received this book and those words about knowing to be silent. I had been turning this matter over for some nights, even before the book returned to me, and I ask myself whether the time has come to fall silent; if the moment has passed and this isn't the place, if this isn't the hour for the mouth to die.

I'm writing you this in the dark of a May dawn; April 30, 1995, Children's Day here in Mexico, is now past. We Mexican children celebrate the day, more often than not, despite the adults. For example, thanks to the supreme government, many indigenous Mexican children celebrate their day in the mountains far from home, in unhygienic conditions. There is no party, but there is great poverty; they have no place to relieve their hunger and despair. The supreme government claims it hasn't expelled these children from their homes; it's only deployed thousands of soldiers in their lands. But with the soldiers came drink, prostitution, robbery, torture, and hostilities. The supreme government says the soldiers have come to defend our "national sovereignty." They're "defending" Mexico against Mexicans. These children haven't been expelled, says the government, and they have no reason to be alarmed by the planes, the tanks, and helicopters, and the thousands of soldiers. They need not be frightened even though the soldiers have orders to arrest and kill their fathers. No, these children haven't been expelled from their homes. They share the mountain's uneven floor out of a desire to be close to their roots. They share mange and malnutrition for the simple pleasure of scratching and showing off their slim figures.

The children of the masters of the government spend the day at parties surrounded by gifts. Zapatista children, masters of nothing if not their own dignity, spend the day at play; they play at war, they play at being soldiers who take back the land that the government has stolen from them, of being farmers who sow their cornfields and gather wood, of being the sick whom no one cures, of being the hungry who must fill their mouths with song instead of food. At night, when the rain and fog press in, they especially like to sing a song that goes something like this:

"Now we can see the horizon,
Zapatista combatant.
The path will be marked
For those who come behind."

And so, for example, Heriberto appears marching in step in the horizon. And coming behind Heriberto, for example, is Oscar's little son, Osmar. The two of them march along, armed with two sticks they've scavenged on a hill nearby. ("They're not sticks," says Heriberto. He assures us that they're carrying powerful weapons capable of destroying the red ant nest near the stream. They bit him and action had to be taken.) Heriberto and Osmar march in line. On the opposite front, Eva advances, armed with a stick that turns into a doll in a less warlike atmosphere. Behind her comes Chelita, whose two years of life raise her a meager few centimeters off the ground, and whose eyes— like those of frightened deer caught in the light—are sure to haunt Heriberto some night in years to come, or whoever lets himself be blinded by their dark gleam. Following Chelita is a puppy so skinny it looks like a tiny marimba.

I'm being told all of this, but just as if I were watching Wellington pitted against Napoleon in the movie *Waterloo* (I think with Orson Welles), and Napoleon is defeated because he has a bellyache. But there is no Orson here, or infantry or artillery support, or defensive formations against cavalry charges. Dispensing with preliminary feints or skirmishes, both Heriberto and Eva have opted for a full frontal attack.

I'm just about to give my opinion that it looks like a battle of the sexes, but Heriberto has already flung himself at Chelita, evading Eva's direct charge, so that she suddenly runs up against an unsuspecting Osmar, who's much less prepared for face-to-face combat, since he's off to one side, in the bushes pooping. Eva declares that he's been scared shitless, but Osmar doesn't say a thing back because he wants to ride the puppy that has been drawn over by the smell. Meanwhile, Chelita has been crying ever since she saw Heriberto coming at her, and now he doesn't know how to quiet her down, so he offers her a stone as a prize ("It's not just a stone," says Heriberto, assuring her she's looking at pure gold). While Chelita keeps on screaming, I'm thinking that they give Heriberto a dose of his own medicine, when Eva arrives in a maneuver known as "shifting the enemy position." She falls on Heriberto from behind. Heriberto has just offered Chelita his anti-red-ant weapon, which Chelita is considering in between sobs...

Eva's doll weapon crashes down on Heriberto's head—Take that!—and the screaming goes stereo (because Chelita, excited by Heriberto's screams, doesn't want to fall behind). And now there's blood and already someone's mother—I don't know whose—is on the way with a belt in hand, and both armies disband and desert the field. In the infirmary, they announce that since Heriberto has a lump the size of an egg and Eva is unscathed, the women have won this battle of the sexes. Heriberto complains of referee bias and prepares his counterattack, but it will have to wait for tomorrow because right now there are beans to eat that don't quite fill the plate, or his belly...

And that's how they spent Chidren's Day, say the children of a settlement called Guadalupe Tepeyac. They spent it in the mountains because in their town there are several thousand soldiers defending the "national sovereignty." And Heriberto says that when he grows up, he's going to be a truck driver and not an airplane pilot, because if you blow a tire on the truck, you just climb down and go on walking, but if you blow a tire on the airplane, there's nowhere to go. And I tell myself that when I grow up I'm going to be an Uruguayan-Argentine and a writer, in that order, and don't think it's going to be easy, because I can't stand the stuff they call *maté*.

But that's not what I wanted to tell you. What I wanted to tell you is a story for you to recount...

Old Don Antonio taught me that you are as big as the enemies you choose to fight, and as small as the fear is big. "Choose a big enemy, and it will make you grow so you can confront him. Lessen your fear because if it grows, it will make you small," Old Don Antonio told me one rainy afternoon, in the hour when tobacco and words reign. The government fears the Mexican people; that's why it needs so many soldiers and police. Its fear is very big. Consequently, it is very small. We're afraid of oblivion, which we have made smaller with our pain and blood. Consequently, we are big.

Put this in one of your writings. Say that Old Don Antonio told you all this.

We've all had an Old Don Antonio at some point. But if you've never had one, you may borrow mine this time.

Tell them how the indigenous communities of the Mexican Southeast lessen their fear in order to make themselves big, and choose colossal enemies to make themselves grow stronger.

That's the idea. I'm sure you'll find better words to convey this. Pick a rainy night with lightning and wind, and you'll see how the story will slip out just like a little drawing that begins to dance and stirs the heart. That's why there are dances and hearts.

OK. *Salud*, and a little smiling face, like the ones with which you sign your letters.

From the mountains of the Mexican Southeast,
Subcomandante Insurgente Marcos.

P.S....POSING AS POLICE NOTICE. It is my duty to inform you that I'm a criminal according to the supreme government of Mexico. Therefore, my correspondence can incriminate you. I beg you to memorize the damning contents of this letter—that is, the appeal of the indigenous villages—and destroy the evidence immediately. If paper was chewing gum, I'd advise you to chew it up and make one of those bubbles that so outrage a good conscience and show a decided lack of breeding and education among those who make them. Although some blow them hoping one of those little bubbles will be big enough to carry us to that path shining there above us, stretching in pain and hope across the sky of our America.

P.P.S....WHICH IS UNLIKELY. If you should see Benedetti, please give him my regards. Please tell him I whispered words of his into a woman's ear and they took her breath away. Words like that move all humanity...

LETTER TO JOHN BERGER

MEXICO, MAY 12, 1995

Heriberto, Eva, and the image of an English Countryside

To: John Berger
High Savoy, France

I.

A reader could ask himself: What is the relationship between the writer and the place and peoples about whom he writes?
—John Berger, *Pig Earth*

Agreed, but he could also ask himself: What is the relationship between a letter written in the jungle of Chiapas, Mexico, and the response that it receives from the French countryside? Or, even better, what is the relationship between the slow beating of the wings of the heron with the hovering of the eagle over a serpent?

For example, in Guadalupe Tepeyac (now a village empty of civilians and filled with soldiers), the herons took over the night sky of December. There were hundreds of them. "Thousands," says Lieutenant Ricardo, a Tzeltal insurgent who sometimes has a propensity to exaggerate. "Millions," said Gladys who, despite being 12 years old (or precisely because of it), does not want to be left out. "They come every year," says the grandfather while the small flashes of white hover above the village, and maybe disappear towards the east?

Are they coming or going? Are they your herons, Mr. Berger? A winged reminder? Or a greeting filled with premonition? A fluttering of wings of something that resists death?

Because as a result, months later, I read in your letter (in a dog-eared clipping from a newspaper, with the date hidden under a mud stain), and in it (your letter) the wings of dawn are hovering once again in the sky and the people of Guadalupe Tepeyac now live in the mountain and not in the little valley whose lights, I imagine, are of some significance on the navigation maps of the herons.

Yes, I know now that the herons about which you wrote to me fly during the winter from North Africa, and that it is improbable that they have anything to do with those that arrived in December of 1994, in the Lacandon jungle. In addition, grandfather says that every year the disconcerting tour above Guadalupe Tepeyac is repeated. Perhaps southeastern Mexico is an obligatory layover, a necessity, a commitment. Perhaps they were not herons, but fragments of an exploded moon, pulverized in the December jungle.

December 1994

Months later, the indigenous of Southeastern Mexico again reiterated their rebellion, their resistance to genocide, to death... The reason? The supreme government decided to carry out organized crime, the essence of neoliberalism, that money, the god of modernity, had planned. Dozens of thousands of soldiers, hundreds of tons of war materials, millions of lies. The objective? The destruction of libraries and hospitals, of homes and seeded fields of corn and beans, the annihilation of every sign of rebellion. The indigenous Zapatistas resisted, they retreated to the mountains, and they began an exodus that today, even as I write these lines, has not ended. Neoliberalism disguises itself as the defense of a sovereignty which has been sold in dollars on the international market.

Neoliberalism, this doctrine that makes it possible for stupidity and cynicism to govern in diverse parts of the earth, does not allow for inclusion other than to hold on by disappearing. "Die as a social group, as a culture, and above all as a resistance. Then you can be part of modernity," say the great capitalists, from the seats of government, to the indigenous campesinos. These indigenous people irritate the modernizing logic of neo-mercantilism. Their rebellion, their defiance, their resistance, irritates them. The anachronism of their existence within a project of globalization, an economic and political project that, soon, will decide that poor people, all the people in opposition, which is to say, the majority of the population, are obstacles. The armed character of "We are here!" of the Zapatista indigenous people does not matter much to them nor does it keep them awake (a little fire and lead will be enough to end such "imprudent" defiance). What matters to them, and bothers them, is that their very existence, in the moment that they [the indigenous Zapatistas] speak out and are heard, is converted into a reminder of an embarrassing omission of "neoliberal modernity": "These Indians should not exist today, we should have put an end to them BEFORE. Now annihilating them will be more difficult, which is to say, more expensive." This is the burden which weighs upon the born again neoliberal government in Mexico.

"Let's resolve the causes of the uprising," say the government negotiators (leftists of yesterday, the shamed of today), as if they were saying: "All of you should not exist, all of this is an unfortunate error of modern history." "Let's resolve the causes" is the elegant synonym for "we will eliminate them." For this system which concentrates wealth and power and distributes death and poverty, the campesinos, the indigenous, do not fit in the plans and projects. They have to be gotten rid of, just like the herons... and the eagles... have to be gotten rid of.

II.

Mystery is not what can be hidden deliberately, but rather, as I have
already shown, the fact that the gamut of the possible can always
surprise us. And this is hardly ever represented. The campesinos do
not present papers as do urban personalities. This is not because they
are "simple," or more sincere, or less astute; simply the space between
that which is unknown of a person and what all the world knows of
him—and this is the space of all representation—it is extremely small.

—JOHN BERGER, *Pig Earth*

A cold dawn drags itself between the fog and the thatched roofs
of the village. It is morning. The dawn goes, the cold remains.
The little paths of mud begin to fill with people and animals.
The cold and a little footpath accompany me in the reading of
Pig Earth. Heriberto and Eva (five and six years old respectively)
come and grab (they "snatched" I should say, but I don't know
if the distinction is understood in English) the book. They look
at the drawing on the front cover (it is a Madrid edition from
1989). It is a copy of a painting by John Constable, an image of
an English countryside. The cover of your book, Mr. Berger,
summons a rapid connection between image and reality. For
Heriberto, for example, there is no doubt that the horse in the
painting is La Muñeca [The Doll] (a mare that accompanied us
in the long year during which the indigenous rebellion governed southeastern Mexico), which no one could mount except
Manuel, a playmate who was twice the age, size, and weight of
Heriberto, who was Chelita's brother, and consequently, also his

future brother-in-law. And what Constable called a "river" was really a river bed, a river bed that crossed through La Realidad / Reality ("La Realidad / Reality" is the name of a village, a reality of which is the limit of Heriberto's horizons. The farthest place that his trips and running around has taken him is La Realidad / Reality).

Constable's painting did not remind Heriberto and Eva of the English countryside. It did not take them outside of the Lacandon jungle. It left them here, or it brought them back. It brought them back to their land, their place, to their being children, to their being campesinos, to their being indigenous people, to their being Mexicans and rebels. For Heriberto and Eva, Constable's painting is a colored drawing of "La Muñeca" and the title, *Scene on a Navigable River,* is not a valid argument: the river is the river bed of "La Realidad/Reality," the horse is the mare La Muñeca, Manuel is riding, and his sombrero fell off, and that's it, on to another book. This time it is about Van Gogh and for Eva and Heriberto, the paintings of Holland are scenes from their land, of their being campesinos. After this Heriberto tells his mother that he spent the morning with the Sup. "Reading big books," says Heriberto, and I believed that this earned him a free hand with a box of chocolate cookies. Eva was more far-sighted, and asked me if I didn't have a book about her doll with the little red bandanna.

III.

The act of writing is nothing more than the act of approximating the experience of what is being written about; in the same manner, it is hoped that the act of reading the written text is another act of similar approximation.

—JOHN BERGER

Or of distancing, Mr. Berger. The writing, and above all the reading of the written text could be an act of distancing. "The written word and the image," says my other, who to add problems paints himself, alone. I think the "reading" of the written word and the image could approximate the experience or distance it. And so, the photographic image of Alvaro, one of the dead combatants in Ocosingo in January 1994, returns. Alvaro returns in the photo, Alvaro with his death speaks in the photo. He says, he writes, he shows: "I am Alvaro, I am indigenous, I am a soldier, I took up arms against being forgotten. Look. Listen. Something is happening in the closing of the 20th century that is forcing us to die in order to have a voice, to be seen, to live." And from the photo of dead Alvaro, a reader from afar could approximate the indigenous situation in modern Mexico, NAFTA, the international forums, the economic bonanza, the first world.

"Pay attention! Something is evil in the macroeconomic plans, something is not functioning in the complicated mathematical calculations that sing the successes of neoliberalism," says Alvaro with his death. His photo says more, his death speaks, his body on the soil of Chiapas takes voice, his head resting in a pool of blood: "Look! This is what the numbers and the speeches hide. Blood, cadavers, bones, lives and hopes, crushed, squeezed dry, eliminated in order to be incorporated into the 'indices of profit and economic growth.'" "Come!" says Alvaro. "Come close! Listen!"

But Alvaro's photo also can "be read" from a distance, as a vehicle which serves to create distance in order to stay on the other side of the photo, like "reading" it in a newspaper in another part of the world. "This did not happen here," says the reader of the photo, "this is Chiapas, Mexico, a historical accident, remedial, forgettable, and... far away." There are, in addition, other readers who confirm it: public announcements, economic figures, stability, peace. This is the use of the indigenous war at the end of the century, to revalue "peace." Like a stain stands out on the object that is stained. "I am here and this photo happened over there, far away, small," says the "reader" who distances himself.

And I imagine, Mr. Berger, that the final result of the relationship between the writer and the reader, through the text ("or from the image," insists my other self again), escapes both. Something is imposed on them, gives significance to the text, provokes one to come closer or go farther away. And this "something" is related to the new division of the world, with the democratization of death and misery, with the dictatorship of power and money, with the regionalization of pain and despair, with the internationalization of arrogance and the market. But it also has to do with the decision of Alvaro (and of thousands of indigenous along with him) to take up arms, to fight, to resist, to seize a voice that they were denied before, to not devalue the cost of the blood that this implies.

And it also has to do with the ear and eye that are opened by Alvaro's message, whether they see and hear it, whether they understand it, whether they draw near to him, his death, his blood that flooded the streets of a city that has always ignored him, always...until this past January first. It also has to do with the eagle and heron, the European peasant who resists being absorbed and the indigenous Latin American rebelling against being killed. It has to do with the panic of the powerful, as the trembling grows in their guts, no matter how strong and power-ful they appear, when, without knowing, they prepare to fall...

And it has to do with—I reiterate and salute it in this way—the letters that come from you to us, and those that, with these lines, bring you these words: the eagle received the message and understood, he understood the approach of the hesitant flight of the heron. And there below, the serpent trembles and fears the morning...

OK, Mr. Berger. *Salud,* and follow closely the heron in the sky, until it appears as a small and passing flash of light, a flower lifting itself up...

From the mountains of Southeastern México,
Subcomandante Insurgente Marcos.

LETTER TO ERIC JAUFFRET
JUNE 20, 1995

To: Eric Jauffret
France

> *I have seen Siqueiros mask the children and incite the walls to rebellion,*
> *and Rivera free the enigmatic, anonymous, and tender accomplice...*
>
> –ERIC JAUFFRET

On the other hand, I have seen our own cover their faces in order to show them to the world, and take off their ski masks in order to hide from the enemy. For example, during a recent arrival of fresh government troops, one of the officials said goodbye to the townspeople. He sent greetings to the Zapatistas. "I will return," he said, "in four months." During those four months he looked for the Zapatistas and did not find them. "They left the mountain and have come into the towns. We'll never be able to find them," says the official, explaining in his own way, that he is involved in an absurd war where the enemy shows himself by hiding, and hides by showing himself.

I've also seen that Beto (10 years old, going on 11 and a half, and a quarter to 12) has turned the world on its head. As proof, he sent me a drawing made with worn-out colored pencils, where the ocean is the sky and the sky is the ocean. Beto is, in terms of work in the community, old now. He carries his share of firewood and has already complicated the life of one of the women in the peace camps. "What is the ocean about?" Beto asks, and searches for an answer in books full of photos, drawings, and letters. The explanations begin to answer the question, that, according to the volunteer teacher, is very important to Beto: Is the ocean a "he" or a "she?" Beto only wants to know if helicopters and planes can fly in the ocean. "No, they can't," the teacher answers and continues a complicated explanation about density, the laws of physics, aerodynamics, the chemical composition of water, and other rules of grammar.

Beto sends a message with his uncle so that among the demands of the EZLN, there is also one about raising the ocean to the sky, and lowering the sky into the ocean. Beto thinks that this way the ocean will be more democratic, because everyone will be able to see it and that he, Beto, will no longer have to suffer through long explanations in order to learn that the "ocean," like "hope," is female. Beto also says that he has a friend called Nabor. Nabor's father died on February 10th, 1995, when the government sent its troops in to recover the "national sovereignty." Mortally wounded, he was separated from his unit, which retreated, in order not to confront the federal troops. Hovering vultures pointed out, days later, where he lay. Beto has adopted Nabor, and has shown him all he needs to know to survive in the Lacandon Jungle. The prodigious student Nabor, brags about how he has already kissed a compañera.

"Mmmm, delicious!" Nabor says as he brings his hand to his lips and gives it a mock kiss.

Nabor agrees with Beto that the sky should be below and the ocean above. A helicopter with artillery passes by in order to confirm it. Beto thinks the change will not be too complicated. They're both blue, right? Both big? "Anyway," Nabor says, "it's simpler to change the world than for us to learn how to walk on our heads." For Beto and Nabor, happiness would be stooping in order to see the sky.

Oh, I forgot. Nabor is three years old, and, as is obvious, over here each year equals a decade, and the classes for "responsible sex" should begin at age 2...

But Mister Jauffret, I am not writing to tell you about Beto's drawing or about his friend Nabor and his plans to turn the world upside down. I am writing to thank you for your letter and to tell you about our actual situation.

The indigenous peoples who support our just cause have decided to resist without surrender, without accepting the alms with which the supreme government hopes to buy them. And they have decided this because they have made theirs a word which is not understood with the head, which cannot be studied or memorized. It is a word which is lived with the heart, a word which is felt deep inside your chest and which makes men and women proud of belonging to the human race. This word is

DIGNITY. Respect for ourselves, for our right to be better, our right to struggle for what we believe in, our right to live and die according to our ideals. Dignity cannot be studied; you live it or it dies. It aches inside you and teaches you how to walk. Dignity is the international homeland we often forget about.

Our ideals are simple, and for that reason very large: we want, for all the men and women of this country, and of the entire world, three things which are fundamental for any human being: democracy, liberty, and justice and a powerful media certainly helps this appearance, that these three things are not the same thing for an indigenous person of the Mexican Southeast as for a European. But it is about the same thing: the right to have a good government, the right to think and act with a freedom that does not imply the slavery of others, and the right to give and receive what is just.

For these three values, for democracy, liberty, and justice, we rose up in arms on January 1st of 1994. For these three values, we resist today without surrender. Both things, the war and resistance, mean that these three values represent everything for us, represent a cause worth fighting for, worth dying for...so that living is worthy of us. Our cause, we believe, is not only ours. It belongs to any honest man or woman in any part of the world. And this is why we aspire for our voice to be heard in all the world, and that our struggle will be taken up by everyone in the world. Our cause is not the cause of war, or the cause of destruction, or the cause of death. Our cause is that of peace, but peace with justice; it is the cause of construction, but with equity and reason; it is the cause of life, but with dignity, and always new, and better.

Today, we find ourselves in a very difficult situation. The war is dressed in its terrible suit of hunger and entire communities suffer in conditions below the minimum level for survival. We willingly accept this, but not because we like martyrdom or sterile sacrifice. We accept it because we know that brothers and sisters the world over will know how to extend their hand to help us triumph in a cause that is theirs as well.

Like yesterday, we cover our faces in order to show the world the true face of the Mexico of the basement; and after washing the mirror with our blood, Mexicans can see their own dignity. Now we hide our face in order to escape the treachery and death that walks in the steps of those who say they govern the country. We are not fighting with our weapons. Our example and our dignity now fight for us.

In the peace talks the government delegates have confessed that they have studied in order to learn about dignity and that they have been unable to understand it. They ask the Zapatista delegates to explain what is dignity. The Zapatistas laugh—after months of pain they laugh. Their laughter echoes and escapes over the high wall behind which arrogance hides its fear. The Zapatista delegates laugh, even when the dialogue ends and they are giving their report.

Everyone who hears them laughs, and the laughter recomposes faces that have been hardened by hunger and betrayal. The Zapatistas laugh in the mountains of the Mexican Southeast and the sky cannot avoid infection by that laughter, and the peals of laughter echo. The laughter is so great that tears rise and it begins to rain as though the laughter were a gift for the dry land...

With so much laughter raining, who can lose? Who deserves to lose?

OK, Mister Jauffret.

Salud, and remember: "The world is as blue as an orange."

From the mountains of the Mexican Southeast,
Subcomandante Insurgente Marcos.

MEXICO: THE MOON BETWEEN THE MIRRORS OF THE NIGHT AND THE CRYSTAL OF THE DAY

I want you for a crystal, never a mirror.

–PEDRO SALINAS

May of 1985. Dawn. The moon peers at the mirror of the lake with jealousy, the lake wrinkles its face with its waves. In the middle of the trajectory between one side and the other, we venture in a canoe that has the same firmness as my decision to cross the lake. Old Man Antonio has invited me to test his canoe. For the past 28 nights, from the new to the full moon, Old Man Antonio has worked, with machete and ax, a large cedar trunk. The vessel is seven meters long. Old Man Antonio explains that canoes can be made of cedar, mahogany, huanacastle, bariy, and he points out the different trees he names. Old Man Antonio is determined to point them out, but I can't tell them apart; they are all large trees as far as I'm concerned. That was during the day; now it is dawn, and as usual we are here navigating in this little wooden cedar vessel which Old Man Antonio has baptized "The Troublemaker." "In honor of the moon," says Old Man Antonio, while he rows with a large and thick stick. Now we are in the middle of the lake. The wind paints curls on the water, and the canoe rises and falls. Old Man Antonio decides he should wait until the wind dies down, and he allows the vessel to coast.

"These waves cannot turn the canoe over," he says, as his cigarette makes smoke spirals much as the wind makes waves.

The moon is full, and in its light it is possible to see the large islets which dot the Miramar lake. Through a smoke spiral, Old Man Antonio calls up an old story.

I'm worried about sinking, which appears imminent (I can't decide whether to be nauseous or terrified), so I'm not in the mood for fables or stories. This, of course, is neither here nor there for Old Man Antonio. Reclined on the bottom of the canoe, he begins to weave his tale...

THE MIRRORS' TALE

The oldest of the elders say that the moon was born right here, in the jungle. They say that a long time ago, the gods had overslept, tired of playing and doing so much. The world was silent. But a soft cry was heard up there in the mountain. Seems like the gods had forgotten a lake and left it in the middle of the mountain. When they divided up the things of the Earth, the little lake was left over, and since they did not know where else to put it, they just left it there, in the midst of so many hills that no one could find it. So the little lake was crying because it was alone. And its cries were such that the heart of the Mother Cedar, who is the sustainer of the world, was saddened by the cries of the little lake. Gathering its large white petticoat, the Cedar came near the little lake.

"What is wrong with you now?" The Cedar asked the water, which was becoming a puddle, because of its incessant crying.

"I don't want to be alone," said the little lake.

"All right, then I will remain at your side," said the Cedar, the sustainer of the world.

"I don't want to be here," said the little lake.

"All right, then you will come with me," said the Cedar.

"No, I want to be down there, close to the earth. I want to be tall. Like you," said the little lake.

"All right, then I will lift you up to the level of my head. But only for a little while, because the wind is mischievous and I might drop you," said the Cedar.

As it could, the Mother Cedar gathered up its petticoat and bent over to take the little lake in its arms. Carefully, because it is the mother, the sustainer of the world, the Cedar placed the little lake on the crown of its head. The Mother Cedar moved slowly, being careful not to spill one drop of water of the lake, because the Mother Cedar could see that the little lake was very thin.

From above the little lake exclaimed: "It is such a joy being up here! Take me to see the world! I want to see all of it!"

"The world is very large, little girl, and you can fall from up there," said the Cedar.

"I don't care! Take me!," the little lake insisted and it pretended to cry.

Mother Cedar did not want the little lake to cry so much, so it began to walk, very straight, with her on its head. Since then the women have learned to walk with a pitcher full of water on their heads so that not a drop falls. Like the Mother Cedar walk women of the jungle when they bring the water from the brook. With a straightened back, their head raised, their step like clouds in the summer. That is how the women in the mountains walk when they are taking the water that heals.

Mother Cedar was good at walking, because in those days the trees were not stationary. They walked from one place to another, making children and filling the world with trees. But the wind was around there, whistling with boredom. So it saw Mother Cedar and wanted to play by lifting its petticoats with a slap. But the Cedar became angry and said: "Be still, wind! Don't you see that I have upon my head a stubborn and weepy lake?"

Then the wind finally saw the little lake, who peered at it from the curly crown of the Cedar. The wind thought the little lake was pretty and decided to flirt with it. So the wind rose up to the head of the Cedar and began to speak pretty words in the ear of the little lake. The little lake quickly preened itself and said to the wind: "If you take me around the world, then I will go with you!"

The wind didn't think twice. It made a horse of clouds and put the little lake on the rump and took the little lake away, so quickly that Mother Cedar did not even notice when the little lake was taken from her head.

The little lake traveled for a good long time with the wind. And the wind told the little lake how pretty it was, how darned cute it was, that any thirst would be quenched with the water of the little lake, that anyone would love sinking inside her, and many other things were said by the wind in order to convince the little lake to make love in a corner of the dawn. And the little lake believed all that was said to her and each time they passed a puddle of water or a lake, the little lake took advantage of its reflection and fixed its wet hair and blinked her liquid eyes and made flirtatious features out of the little waves on her round face.

But the little lake only wanted to go from one end of the world to the other, nothing about making love in a corner of the dawn. The wind became bored and took her very high and shied away with a loud neigh and threw the little lake and the little lake began falling but since it was so high it took much time and surely it would have hurt itself if some stars had not caught sight of it and hooked it to their points. Seven stars took it by the sides, and like a sheet, raised it once again into the sky. The little lake was pale because it was so frightened of falling. And since she no longer wanted to return to the earth, she asked to stay with the stars.

"All right," said the stars, "but you will have to come with us wherever we go."

"Yes," answered the little lake, "I will go with you."

But the little lake was saddened to always take the same route and she began to cry again. Her crying awoke the gods and they went to see what was happening or where the crying came from and they saw the little lake, being pulled by the seven stars, crossing the night. When they learned the story, the gods were angry because they had not made lakes so they could wander in the sky, but so that they stayed on earth. They went to see the little lake and said to it: "You will no longer be a lake. Lakes do not live in the sky. But since we cannot take you down, then you will remain here. But we will call you 'moon' and your punishment, because you are vain and a flirt, will be to reflect the well where the light is put away on earth."

Apparently, the gods had put away the light inside the earth and had made a large round hole so that whenever the light and the spirit diminished in the stars they could come and drink there. So the moon has no light, it is only a mirror, and when it appears full, its front reflects the great hole filled with light, where the stars drink. Mirror of light, that is what the moon is. So whenever the moon strolls in front of a lake, the mirror looks into a mirror. And even so, the moon is never happy or angry, it is the troublemaker...

The gods also punished Mother Cedar for being such a pamperer. They no longer allowed it to walk from one place to the other, and they gave it the world to carry, and doubled the thickness of its skin so it would not respond to any crying it might hear. Since then, the Cedar has skin of stone and stands without moving. If the Cedar moves, even a little, the world will fall.

"So it happened," said Old Man Antonio. Since then the moon reflects the light which is stored inside the Earth. That is why when it finds a lake, the moon stops to fix its hair and face. That is why whenever women pass a mirror, they stop to look at themselves. That was a gift from the gods; to each woman was given a piece of moon, so they could fix their hair and their face and so they would not want to travel and climb to the sky.

Old Man Antonio stopped, but the wind did not, the waves continued to threaten the little boat. But I said nothing. Not because I was reflecting upon the words of Old Man Antonio, but because I was sure, that if I opened my mouth, I would expel even my liver onto the agitated mirror in which the moon rehearses its flirtatiousness.

I. WITHIN THE NIGHT OF RANCOR AND CONFUSION

In Mexico, sometimes the moon is painted in a resplendent red. Neither blush nor blood, it is rage and rancor that illuminate its pearly face. Upon its return from its long voyage through the Mexican night, the moon ends its repeated path of mirrors and returns to its tired walk. Its look is red...because of its rancor... and confusion...

Why? What has it seen? Stammering, annoyed and with a thin, thready voice which seems like a spiral of wind in May, the moon tells the story of its last voyage. It says it walked the Mexican night, and that, as it tumbled in the giant labyrinth of mirrors which is our contemporary history, it came to...

Subcomandante Insurgente Marcos

SUBCOMMANDANTE MARCOS' LETTER TO THE PEOPLE OF THE U.S.
SEPTEMBER 13, 1995

The U.S. government has been wrong more than once with regard to its foreign policy. When this has occurred, it is due to the fact it had made a mistake as to the man it ought to be backing. History is not lacking in these types of examples. In the first half of this decade, the U.S. government made a mistake backing Carlos Salinas de Gortari. It made a mistake signing NAFTA, which lacked a majority support from the North American people, and it meant an order of summary execution against the Mexican indigenous people.

On the dawn of 1994, we rose up in arms. We rose up, not seeking power, nor responding to a foreign order. We rose up to say: "Here we are." The Mexican government, our government, had forgotten us and was ready to perpetrate a genocide without bullets or bombs, it was ready to annihilate us with the quiet death of sickness, misery, and oblivion. The U.S. government became the accomplice of the Mexican government in this genocide.

With the signing of NAFTA, the U.S. government acted as guarantor of and gave its blessing to the murder of millions of Mexicans. *Did the people of the U.S. know this?* Did they know that its government was signing accords of massive extermination in Mexico? Did the people of the U.S. know that their government was backing a criminal? That man is gone. We remained. Our demands have not been met and our arms keep waving "here we are" to the new government, to the people of Mexico, to the people and governments of the world. We waited patiently for the new government to listen to us and pay attention to us. But, within the dark circles of U.S. power someone decided that we, the insurgent indigenous of the Mexican Southeast, were the worst threat to the United States of America. From the darkness came the order: Finish them!

They put a price on our brown skin, on our culture, on our word, on our uprising. The U.S. government decided, once more, to back a man, someone who continues with the politics of deceit of his predecessor, someone who denies the people of Mexico democracy, freedom, and justice. Millions of dollars were lent to that man and his government. Without the approval of the American people, an enormous loan, without precedent in history, was granted to the Mexican government. Not to improve the living conditions of the people, not for the democratization of the country's political life, not for the economic reactivation promoting factories and productive projects. This money is for speculation, for corruption, for simulation, for the annihilation of a group of rebels, Indians for the most part, poorly armed, poorly nourished, ill equipped, but very dignified, very rebellious, and very human.

So much money to finance deceit can only be explained by fear. But, what does the U.S. government fear? Truth? That the North American people realize that their money is helping to back the oldest dictatorship in the modern world? That the North American people realize that their taxes pay for the persecution and death of the Mexican indigenous population? What are the North American people afraid of? Ought the people of North America fear our wooden rifles, our bare feet, our exhausted bodies, our language, our culture? Ought the North American people fear our scream in demand of democracy, liberty, and justice? Aren't these three truths the foundation which brought forth the birth of the United States of America? Aren't democracy, liberty, and justice rights that belong to all human beings?

How many millions of dollars justify that one may deny, to any human being, anywhere in the world, his right to be free in the thoughts that bring about words and actions, free to give and receive that which he justly deserves, to freely elect those who govern him and enforce collective goals? Should the North American people on the other hand fear money, modern weapons, the sophisticated technology of drug-trafficking? Should the North American people fear the complicity between drug trafficking and governments? Should the North American people fear the consequences of the single party dictatorship in Mexico? Should it fear the violence that the lack of freedom, democracy, and justice usually brings about irrevocably?

Today, the U.S. government, which for decades prided itself on promoting democracy in the world, is the main support of a dictatorship which, born at the beginning of the 20th Century, wants to end this century with the same lie, governing against the will of the Mexican people. Sooner or later, in spite of the support of the U.S. government, in spite of the millions of dollars, in spite of the tons of lies, the dictatorship that darkens the Mexican sky will be erased. The people of Mexico will find the ways to achieve the democracy, liberty, and justice that is their historical right.

Americans: The attacks against the Mexican nation brought about by U.S. political personalities have been big and numerous. In their analysis, they point out the awkwardness and corruption of the Mexican government (an awkwardness and corruption which have increased and are maintained under the shadow of the U.S. government's support) and they identify them with an entire people who take shelter under the Mexican flag. They are wrong.

Mexico is not a government. Mexico is a nation which aspires to be sovereign and independent, and in order to be that, must liberate itself from a dictatorship and raise on its soil the universal flag of democracy, liberty, and justice. Fermenting racism, fear, and insecurity, the great personalities of U.S. politics offer economic support to the Mexican government so that it controls by violent means the discontent against the economic situation. They offer to build more border walls, pretending to put a stop to the search for a better life for millions of Mexicans at their northern border.

The best wall against massive immigration to the U.S. is a free, just, and democratic regime in Mexico. If Mexicans could find in their own land what now is denied them, they would not be forced to look for work in other countries. By supporting the dictatorship of the State party system in Mexico, whatever the name of the man or the party, the North American people are supporting an uncertain and anguishing future. By supporting the people of Mexico in their aspirations for democracy, liberty, and justice, the North American people honor their history...and their human condition.

Today, in 1995 and after twenty years and tens of thousands of dead and wounded, the American government recognizes that it made a mistake getting involved in the Vietnam War. Today, in 1995, the U.S. government has begun to get involved in the Mexican government's dirty war against the Zapatista population. War, material support, military advisors, undercover actions, electronic espionage, financing, diplomatic support, CIA activities. Little by little, the U.S. government is beginning to get involved in an unfair war condemned to failure for those who are carrying it on, the Mexican government. Today, in 1995 and 20 years before 2015, it is possible to stop and not to repeat the error of other years. It is not necessary to wait until 2015 for the U.S. government to recognize that it was an error to get involved in the war against the Mexican people.

It is time for the people of the U.S. to keep its historical agreement with respect to its neighbor to the South. To no longer make a mistake as to which man to support. To support not a man but a people, the Mexican people in their struggle for democracy, liberty, and justice. History will signal, implacable, on which side were the people and the government of the U.S. On the side of dictatorship, of a man, of reaction; or on the side of democracy, of a people, of progress.

Salud, and long life to the people of the United States of America.

From the Mexican Southeast,
Subcomandante Insurgente Marcos.
Mexico, September 13, 1995.
(20 years before...)

A CALL TO LATIN AMERICA
MARCH 10, 1996

To Latin America, in the pain-filled South of the American continent,
Planet Earth (seventh planet of the solar system if you're counting from
beyond, like from that star that's up there, above... no, not that one, the
other one... and were walking toward the sun, the same way that you
walk inward, with fear and hope):

Suppose it isn't true that there's no alternative.

Suppose impunity and harm aren't the only future.

Suppose it's possible that the thin line separating war and peace won't grow ever narrower.

Suppose that some madmen and romantics believe that another world, another life, is possible.

Suppose the worst, that these madmen believe there are others, more madmen who think like them.

Suppose the inadmissible, that all of these madman want to join together.

Suppose that they suppose from this meeting of madmen, some measure of reason will emerge.

Wouldn't you like to attend such a mad meeting of suppositions?

Yes? No? If you suppose you'd answer no, then get serious, don't bother reading the following paragraphs, and write "Wrong Address" somewhere in the margin.

Don't bother returning this to the sender.

If you suppose you'd answer yes, do something useful with this invitation: start a fire, make a paper plane or a paper doll, something that will make you smile. If beyond supposing that you'd like to go, you suppose that you'd like to attend this meeting, and may even try to go to it, then read on.

If you're already not too dizzy, it may interest you to know that the Pan-American Meeting for Humanity and Against Neoliberalism will be taking place in La Realidad (Reality). Isn't that charming? Now that we have our suspicions, suppositions, and suppositories and you suppose that you are attending, we suppose that you'll want to know when and how.

We'd like you to accept our invitation so those April days can witness history being induced to rebel; to shake itself up and wake itself up and change its course so it can accompany us to the Pan-American Meeting for Humanity against Neoliberalism. As the law of these times dictates, we'll be in La Realidad (Reality), one of those corners of southeastern Chiapas where pain is transformed into hope thanks to the complicated chemistry of dignity and rebellion.

The days? Yes, they're usually denoted on calendars as 3, 4, 5, 6, 7, and 8 of April of the year we are enduring, 1996.

The "how" has a few details we won't include here, so as to not spoil your lunch or ruin your excitement at discovering the existence of this meeting, that this invitation presupposes. So we'll leave the details to the committee chairwoman, if she can find them.

Good. Now, when someone is supposedly looking for you, you have the option of hiding, or concurring that you're both looking for the same thing, because at this kind of meeting it's better to take the initiative. Just so you know, please pack the necessary pencil (in case you get the opportunity to write something), colored paper of various sizes (so if no one pays attention, you can at least make little paper dolls), a good length of string (so if you stray from the meeting you can find the way back–where?), and patience and discretion.

Around here we're expert at hoping, but will you make it?

OK. *Salud*, and while we're on the subject, here's hoping we make history before history makes it for us.

From the wilds of the Mexican Southeast,
Subcomandante Insugente Marcos.

Did you notice the invitation's cold, formal tone? Doesn't this transgressor of the law begin this *veeery* important international event with wondrous gravity? Doesn't this invitation at least deserve a simple "yes," or "no," or "I don't know" RSVP sent via the only secure conduit, i.e. a paper plane? No, don't worry; the wind knows which way to blow and carry your reply to us, if we can be found at all...

SECOND DECLARATION OF LA REALIDAD (REALITY) FOR HUMANITY, AND AGAINST NEOLIBERALISM
AUGUST 1996

Words of the Zapatista Army of National Liberation in the closing act of the First Intercontinental Encounter for Humanity and Against Neoliberalism [*read by Subcomandante Insurgente Marcos*].

Through my voice speaks the voice of the Zapatista Army of National Liberation. La Realidad (Reality), Planet Earth. August 3rd, 1996.

Brothers and sisters of the whole world: Brothers and sisters of Africa, America, Asia, Europe, and Oceania:

Brothers and sisters attending the First Intercontinental Encounter for Humanity and Against Neoliberalism:

Welcome to the Zapatista R/reality. Welcome to this territory in struggle for humanity. Welcome to this territory in rebellion against neoliberalism.

The Zapatistas greet all who attended this encounter. Here, in the mountains of the Mexican Southeast, when a collective greets whoever comes with good words, it is applauded. We ask that everyone greet each other and that everyone greet the delegations from: Italy, Brazil, Great Britain, Paraguay, Chile, Philippines, Germany, Peru, Argentina, Austria, Uruguay, Guatemala, Belgium, Venezuela, Iran, Denmark, Nicaragua, Zaire, France, Haiti, Ecuador, Greece, Japan, Kurdistan, Ireland, Costa Rica, Cuba, Sweden, The Netherlands, South Africa, Switzerland, Spain, Portugal, The United States, The Basque Country, Turkey, Canada, Puerto Rico, Bolivia, Australia, Mauritania, Mexico ["Norway!" and "Colombia!" were called out from the crowd].

Welcome, all men, women, children, and elders from the five continents who have responded to the invitation of the Zapatista indigenous communities to search for hope for humanity, against neoliberalism.

Brothers and sisters:

When this dream, that today awakens in R/reality, began to be dreamed by us, we thought it would be a failure. We thought that, maybe, we could gather a few dozen people from a few countries. We were wrong. As always, we were wrong. It wasn't a few dozen, but thousands of human beings, who came from five continents to find themselves in R/reality, here at the close of the twentieth century.

The word born within these mountains, these Zapatista mountains, found ears that gave it cover, that cared for and launched it anew, so that it might arrive far away and circle the world. The crazy insanity of a convocation of the five continents to reflect critically on our past, our present, and our future, found that it wasn't alone in its delirium, and soon insanities from the whole planet began to work on bringing the dream to rest in Reality, to bathe it in the mud, grow it under the rain, moisten it under the sun, speak it with the others, go drawing it, giving it form and body.

As to what happened during these days, much will be written later. Today we can say that we are certain of at least one thing. A dream dreamed in the five continents can come to make itself real in R/reality. Who now will be able to tell us that dreaming is lovely but futile? Who now will be able to argue that dreams, however many the dreamers, cannot become a reality?

How is joy dreamed in Africa? What marvels walk in the European dream? How many tomorrows does the dream hold in Asia? To what music does the American dream dance? How does the heart speak, that dreams in Oceania?

To whom does it matter how and what we dream here, or in any part of the world? Who are they who dare to combine with their dream, all the dreams of the world? What's happening in the mountains of the Mexican Southeast that finds an echo and mirror in the streets of Europe, in the suburbs of Asia, the rural areas of America, the townships of Africa, and in the homes of Oceania? What's happening with the peoples of these five continents that, so we are all told, only ever encountered each other to make war or compete? Wasn't this turn of the century synonymous with despair, bitterness, and cynicism? From where, and how, did all of these dreams arrive in R/reality?

May Europe tell us of the long bridge that allowed them to span history and the Atlantic Ocean in order to find itself now in R/reality.

May Asia speak and explain the gigantic leap of its heart to arrive and beat in R/reality. May Africa speak and describe the lengthy sailing of its restless image to come and reflect upon itself in R/reality. May Oceania speak and tell of the multiple flights of thought bouncing away until it rested in R/reality. May America speak and remember the increased feeling of its hope to arrive, remembering to the point of renewing itself in R/reality.

May the five continents speak, and everyone listen. May humanity suspend for a moment its silence of shame and anguish. May humanity speak. May humanity listen...

In the world of those who live in the Power and kill for the Power, the human being doesn't fit; there is no space for hope, no place for tomorrow. Slavery, or death, is the alternative that their world offers to all worlds. The world of money, their world, governs from the stock exchanges. Speculation is today the principal source of enrichment and, at the same time, the best demonstration of the atrophy of the human being's capacity to work. Work is no longer necessary in order to produce wealth; now all that's needed is speculation.

Crimes and wars are carried out so that the global stock exchanges may be pillaged by one another.

Meanwhile, millions of women, millions of youth, millions of indigenous people, millions of homosexuals, millions of human beings of all races and colors only participate in the financial markets as a devalued currency worth always less and less, the currency of their blood making profits.

The globalization of markets is erasing borders for speculation and crime, and multiplying them for human beings. Countries are obligated to erase their national borders when it comes to the circulation of money, but to multiply their internal borders.

Neoliberalism doesn't turn many countries into only one country, it turns each one of them into many countries.

The lie of uni-polarity and inter-nationalization turns itself into a nightmare of war, a fragmented war, again and again, so many times that nations are pulverized. In this world that Power is globalizing in order to get around the obstacles in its war of conquest, national governments are turned into military underlings of a new world war against humanity.

From the stupid career of nuclear armament, destined to annihilate humanity in one blow with nuclear weapons, it has gone to the absurd militarization of all aspects of the life of national societies, a militarization destined to annihilate humanity in many blows, in many places, and in many ways. What were formerly known as "national armies" are turning into simple units of a greater army, the one that neoliberalism arms and leads against humanity. The end of the so-called "Cold War" didn't stop the arming of the world, it only changed the model of this mortal merchandising: weapons of all sizes and for all kinds of criminal tastes. More and more, not only are the so-called "institutional" armies armed, but also the armies that drug trafficking builds up to assure its empire. More or less rapidly, national societies are being militarized and the armies supposedly created to protect their borders from foreign enemies are turning their cannons and rifles around and aiming them inward.

It is not possible for neoliberalism to become the world's reality without the argument of death served up by institutional and private armies, without the gag served up by prisons, without the blows and assassinations served up by the military and the police. National repression is the necessary premise for the globalization that neoliberalism imposes.

The more neoliberalism advances as a global system, the more numerous grow the weapons and the ranks of the armies and national police. The numbers of the imprisoned, the disappeared, and the assassinated in different countries also grow.

A world war: the most brutal, the most complete, the most universal, the most effective.

Each country, each city, each rural area, each house, each person, everything is a large or small battleground. On the one side is neoliberalism with all its repressive power and all its machinery of death; on the other side is the human being.

There are those who resign themselves to being one more number in the huge stock—pouch/purse/exchange—of Power. There are those who resign themselves to being slaves. He who is also master to other slaves cynically walks the slave's horizontal ladder. In exchange for the bad life and the crumbs that Power hands out, there are those who sell themselves, resign themselves, surrender themselves. In any part of the world, there are slaves who say they are happy being slaves. In any part of the world there are men and women who stop being human and take their place in the gigantic market that trades in dignities.

But there are those who do not resign themselves, there are those who decide to be uncomfortable, there are those who do not sell themselves, there are those who do not surrender themselves. There are, around the world, those who resist being annihilated in this war. There are those who decide to fight.

In any place in the world, any time, any man or woman rebels to the point of tearing off the clothes that resignation has woven for them, and that cynicism has dyed grey. Any man, any woman, of whatever color in whatever tongue, repeats to himself, to herself, "Enough already"—*Ya Basta*!

Enough already of lies. Enough already of crime. Enough already of death. "Enough already of war," every man and woman repeats to themselves.

In whatever part of any of the five continents that any man or woman eagerly resists Power and instead builds their own, their path then doesn't imply the loss of dignity and hope.

Any man or woman decides whether to live and struggle for their part in history. No longer does Power dictate their steps; no longer does Power administer life and decide death.

Any man or any woman responds to death with life. And responds to the nightmare by dreaming and struggling against war, against neoliberalism, for humanity...

By struggling for a better world all of us are fenced in, threatened with death. The fence is reproduced globally. In every continent, every city, every rural area, every house. Power's fence of war closes in on the rebels whom humanity always thanks.

But fences are broken. In every house, in every rural area, in every city, in every state, in every country, on every continent, the rebels struggle, and the fence shakes.

The rebels seek each other out. They walk towards one another. They find each other, and together break other fences. In the rural areas and cities, in the states, in the nations, on the continents, the rebels begin to recognize themselves, to know themselves to be equal and different. They continue on their tiring walk, walking as it is now necessary to walk, that is to say, struggling...

A R/reality spoke to them then. Rebels from the five continents heard it, and set off walking.

To arrive at the intercontinental R/reality, each one has had to make his own, her own, road. From the five arms of the star of the world, the steps of men and women, whose dignified word searched for a place to be spoken and heard, has arrived at R/reality, the place of the encounter.

It was necessary to break through many fences to arrive and break through the fence around R/reality. There are many different fences. In ours, one must get past the police, customs officials, tanks, cannons, trenches, planes, helicopters, rain, mud, and insects. Each one of the rebels from the five continents has their own fence, own struggle, and a broken fence to add to the memory of other rebels.

This is how the intercontinental encounter began. It was initiated on all the continents, in all the countries, in all the places where any man or woman began to say to themselves, "Enough already!"

Who can say in what precise locale, and at what exact hour and date this intercontinental encounter for humanity and against neoliberalism began? We don't know. But we do know who initiated it. All the rebels around the world started it. Here, we are only a small part of those rebels, it's true. But to all the diverse fences that all the rebels of the world break every day, you have added one more crack, that of the fence around the Zapatista R/reality.

In order to achieve that, you had to struggle against your respective governments and then confront the "fence" of papers and procedures with which the Mexican government thought to stop you. You are all fighters, men and women who break through fences of all kinds. That's why you made it to R/reality. Maybe you can't yet see the greatness of your achievement, but we do see it.

That is why we want to ask your forgiveness for the stupidity of the Mexican government that, by means of its immigration agents, has done everything possible to impede your arrival to these Zapatista lands. These agents of idiocy-made government believe that passports and permits are still necessary in order to speak and listen to dignity. We are sure that all of you will know how to comprehend why this imbecility believes that nationality divides human beings. We ask that you pardon them. After all, we have to thank the Mexican government that has reminded us that we are all different, even though it has done so with this poor exhibition. But we also have to thank the indigenous communities who received us these days, they who have reminded us that we are all equal.

That is why we, the Zapatistas, have proposed to struggle for a better government here in Mexico. We are struggling to have a government that is even a little intelligent, and that understands that dignity won't acknowledge passports, visas, and other absurdities. This is what we are about now, and we will surely achieve it.

But while this is going on, we ask in the name of the indigenous communities that when you pass the immigration checkpoints on your way out, that you do us the favor of congratulating the Mexican government on the success it achieved with the fence they put up around an indigenous rebel movement that, it is plainly evident, only has influence in four small municipalities in the southeastern Mexican state of Chiapas.

Some of the best rebels from the five continents arrived in the mountains of the Mexican Southeast. All of them brought their ideas, their hearts, their worlds. To find themselves among other ideas, other reasons, other worlds, for that, they came to R/reality.

A world made of many worlds found itself in the mountains of the Mexican Southeast. A world made of many worlds opened a space, and established its right to be possible, raised the banner of being necessary, fastened to the middle of the earth's R/reality to announce a better future. A world of all the worlds that rebel and resist Power, a world of all the worlds that inhabit this world opposing cynicism, a world that struggles for humanity, and against neoliberalism. This was the world that we lived in during these days; this is the world that we have found here...

This encounter doesn't end in R/reality. It just so happens that now it must search for a place to continue on.

But what next?

A new number in the useless enumeration of the numerous international orders?

A new scheme that calms and alleviates the anguish of a lack of recipes?

A global program for world revolution?

A theorization of Utopia, so that it can continue to maintain a prudent distance from the reality that anguishes us?

A "flow chart" that assures us all of a position, a task, a title, and no work?

The echo continues, the reflected image of the possible and forgotten: the possibility and necessity of speaking and listening.

Not the echo that fades out, or the force that decreases after its highest apex.

Yes, the echo that breaks barriers and continues.

The echo of small distinction, the local and particular, reverberating in the echo of great distinction, the intercontinental and galactic.

The echo that recognizes the existence of the other and does not overpower or attempt to silence the other.

The echo that takes its place, and speaks its own voice, and speaks the voice of the other.

The echo that reproduces its own sound and opens itself to the sound of the other.

The echo of this rebel voice transforming itself, and renewing itself in other voices.

An echo that turns itself into a network of voices that, before the deafness of Power, opts to speak to itself, knowing itself to be one and many, acknowledging itself to be equal in its desire to listen and be listened to, recognizing itself as different in the tonalities and levels of the voices forming it.

A network of voices that resist the war that Power wages on them.

A network of voices that not only speak, but also struggle and resist for humanity and against neoliberalism.

A network of voices that are born resisting, reproducing their resistance in other even quieter or lonelier voices.

A network that covers the five continents and helps to resist the death that Power promises us.

The great pocket of voices, sounds that search for their place, fitting with others, continues.

The great torn pocket, that keeps the best of itself and opens itself for what's better to be born and to grow, continues.

The mirror-pocket of voices, the world in which sounds may be listened to separately, recognizing their specificity, the world in which sounds may include themselves in one great sound, continues.

The world within the many worlds that continues to be needed.

Humanity, recognizing itself to be plural, different, inclusive, tolerant of itself, with hope, continues.

The network of human and rebel voices on the five continents, continues.

The voices of all the people we are, the voice that speaks this *Second Declaration of Reality for Humanity and Against Neoliberalism* continues.

Brothers and sisters of Africa, Asia, America, Europe, and Oceania:

Considering that we are:

Against the international order of death, against the globalization of war and armaments.

Against dictatorships, against authoritarianism, against repression.

Against the politics of economic liberalization, against hunger, against poverty, against robbery, against corruption.

Against patriarchy, against xenophobia, against discrimination, against racism, against crime, against the destruction of the environment, against militarism.

Against stupidity, against lies, against ignorance.

Against slavery, against intolerance, against injustice, against marginalization, against forgetfulness.

Against neoliberalism.

Considering that we are:

For the international order of hope, for a new, just, and dignified peace.

For a new politics, for democracy, for political liberties.

For justice, for life, and dignified work.

For civil society, for full rights for women in every aspect, for the respect of elders, youth, and children, for the defense and protection of the environment.

For intelligence, for culture, for education, for truth.

For liberty, for tolerance, for inclusion, for having memory.

For humanity.

We declare:

First, that we will make a collective network of all our particular struggles and resistances. An intercontinental network of resistance against neoliberalism, an intercontinental network of resistance for humanity.

This intercontinental network of resistance, recognizing differences and acknowledging similarities, will search to find itself with other resistances around the world. This intercontinental network of resistance will be the medium in which distinct resistances may support one another. This intercontinental network of resistance is not an organizing structure; it doesn't have a central head or decision maker; it has no central command or hierarchies. We are the network, all of us who resist.

Second, that we will make a network of communication among all our struggles and resistances. An intercontinental network of alternative communication against neoliberalism, an intercontinental network of alternative communication for humanity.

This intercontinental network of alternative communication will search to weave the channels so that words may travel all the roads that resist. This intercontinental network of alternative communication will be the medium by which distinct resistances communicate with one another.

This intercontinental network of alternative communication is not an organizing structure, nor has it a central head or decision maker, nor does it have a central command or hierarchies. We are the network, all of us who speak and listen.

This we declare:

To speak and to listen for humanity and against neoliberalism. To resist and struggle for humanity and against neoliberalism.

For the whole world: Democracy! Liberty! Justice! From whatever reality of whichever continent!

Brothers and sisters:

We do not propose that those of us who are present here sign this declaration and that this encounter end today.

We propose that the intercontinental encounter for humanity and against neoliberalism continue on every continent, in every country, in each rural area and city, in each house, school, or workplace where human beings who want a better world live.

The indigenous communities have taught us that to resolve a problem, no matter how great it may be, it is always good to consult all of the people. That is why we propose that this declaration be distributed around the world and that a consultation be carried out, at least in all the countries in attendance, on the following question:

Do you agree to subscribe to the Second Declaration of Reality for Humanity and Against Neoliberalism?

We propose that this "Intercontinental Consultation for Humanity and Against Neoliberalism" be realized on the five continents during the first two weeks of December, 1996.

We propose that we organize this consultation in the same way that this encounter was organized, that all of us who attended and those who couldn't attend but who accompanied us from afar in this encounter, organize and carry out the consultation. We propose that we make use of all the possible and impossible media in order to consult with the greatest number of human beings on the five continents. The intercontinental consultation is part of the resistance we are organizing and one way of making contacts and encounters with other resistances. Part of a new way of doing political work in the world, that is what the intercontinental consultation wants to be.

Not only that. We also propose that we start calling people to the Second Intercontinental Encounter for Humanity and Against Neoliberalism.

We propose that it be carried out in the second half of 1997 and that it be in the European continent. We propose that the exact date and place of the encounter be defined by the brothers and sisters of Europe in a meeting they hold after this first encounter.

We all hope that there will be this second intercontinental encounter and that it be held, of course, on another continent. When this second encounter is held, we want to make it clear from this moment on, that we will find the way to participate directly, wherever it is held.

Brothers and sisters:

We continue to be uncomfortable. What the theorists of neoliberalism tell us is false: that everything is under control, including everything that isn't under control.

We are not the escape valve for the rebellion that could destabilize neoliberalism. It is false that our rebel existence legitimates Power.

Power fears us. That is why it pursues us and fences us in. That is why it jails and kills us.

In R/reality, we are the possibility that it can be defeated and made to disappear.

Maybe there are not so many of us, but we are men and women who struggle for humanity, who struggle against neoliberalism.

We are men and women who struggle around the world.

We are men and women who want for the five continents:

Democracy!
Liberty!
Justice!

From the mountains of the Mexican Southeast,
The Indigenous Revolutionary Clandestine Committee—General
Command of the Zapatista Army of National Liberation.
La Realidad (Reality), Planet Earth, August, 1996.

AN URGENT TELEGRAM
DECEMBER 8, 1996

To the National and International Civil Society

MADAM:

SALUD, GREETINGS. STOP. I BOW TO YOU MANY TIMES. STOP. SUPREME GOVERNMENT WITH AMNESIA. STOP. FORGOTTEN AGREEMENTS. STOP. RENEWED EXCUSES. STOP. PROBABLE NEED FOR MORE INDIGENOUS PEOPLES' BLOOD TO REFRESH MEMORY. STOP. YOUR PRESENCE IS URGENTLY REQUIRED. STOP. AN INTERCONTINENTAL DANCE MAY SERVE TO REFRESH MEMORY. STOP. THE GRAYS HOPE TO WIN. STOP. RAINBOW NEEDED URGENTLY. STOP. IF THERE IS DANCE I WANT ONE. STOP. SIGH. STOP. AFTER YOU. STOP. SIGH. STOP. HAND IN HAND AND HAND ON WAIST. STOP. SIGH. STOP. 1-2-3. STOP. SIGH. OK. STOP. *SALUD*. STOP. MAY THE DANCE PAINT THE SKY ON THE GROUND. STOP.

The Sup, thinking telegraphically and naively that the periods and hyphens mark a beat for dancing and a path for walking.

From the mountains of the Mexican Southeast,
Subcomandante Insurgente Marcos,
CCRI-CG of the EZLN.

Oh, I forgot. In Durito's letter, there's a story I guess I should add to his book, Stories for a Sleepless Solitude, *in the section called "Stories for Deciding." Here goes then:*

The Story of the Live Person and the Dead Person
Once there was a live person and a dead person. And the dead person said to the live person:
"My, I envy your restlessness."
And then the live person said to the dead person:
"My, I envy your tranquility."
And there they were, envying each other, when suddenly a bean-brown horse went by at full gallop.

Ta-dah.

The Moral of the story, I repeat, is that all final options are a trap. It's imperative to find the bean-brown horse.

DON DURITO OF THE LACANDON

(Please send fan letters, requests for interviews, carnations, and signatures of support for the Anti-Big-Boots Beetle Society to Huapac Leaf #69, Mountains of Mexican Southeast [on the side where the Sup lives]. Phone callers, please note: don't worry if the answering machine isn't on. I don't have one.)

DIGNITY AT WHAT PRICE?
NOVEMBER 2, 1995

To: Cecilia Rodriguez
National Commission for Democracy, USA

From: Subcomandante Insurgente Marcos
CCRI-CG of the EZLN
Chiapas, Mexico

Cecilia:

I write these lines to you during this dawn in which the dead, our dead, accept the bridge extended to them through thousands of offerings in the mountains of the Mexican Southeast.

The reason for it is not pleasant; it is not a salute, yet it is a salute.

We want you to know that we repudiate, together with all honest men and women, the criminal intent to which you were subjected. Yes, "subjected," because that kind of aggression consists of making a thing, an object of a human being, and "using" that human being as things get used. Those responsible for the attempt will be hunted. Yes, hunted like animals, which is what they are.

But we also want you to know that we salute your determination, your refusal to be humiliated and converted into what the Powerful call a "normal woman," a conformist, a resigned, quiet, and objectified woman. As you have well pointed out, the aggression against you is part of a "silent" war, a "discreet" war, a war beyond the reach of the headlines in the press and therefore, distant from the financial markets. We salute your wisdom in reminding everyone that here, in this country called Mexico, there is a war, a war by those who would like to preserve irrationality and eternal omnipotence against those who want a democratic change. We salute all of that, this is true. But above all we salute you as a Zapatista woman, your "I will not surrender!," your "I am here!," your "enough is enough!" We salute the fact that being a Zapatista is not limited by borders or customs checkpoints, that it jumps walls and mocks the "border patrol," that it finds voice and a banner in the Latino blood upon which, among others, rests the power of the American Union.

The body of a woman is also a battleground in this "new type" of war designed for extermination. They wound you as a woman, but above all as a Zapatista. And more so, because you are a North American citizen who sympathizes with the EZLN and its cause of peace with democracy, liberty, and justice.

Some women, among which are those who say they are close to Zapatismo, take advantage of the dilemma of rape to denounce... the Zapatista machos! They now demand that we take off our ski-masks, they say, in order to distance ourselves from the rapists and so that we will not promote, they say, crimes such as the one you suffered. We are not the enemy, and our ski-masks do not hide criminals. They remain indignant, they demand a denial, an explanation, a penance for the simple fact that we are men. This is the new crime of which we are accused; of being men. Because of it, they say, we are accomplices of the rapists. Because we have taken up arms, they say, we have created a climate of violence against women.

But this is not a position common to everyone. The great majority of women close to Zapatismo (in other words, close to you) understand that this crime forms a part of a belligerent chain which has found in the body of a woman a battleground. They and we understand that it is the political, economic, social, and cultural system which holds up as its banners crime and impunity, which promotes, nurtures, protects, and permits this and other aggressions. We understand, they and us, that we should fight to transform the entire world into something better: a world with democracy, liberty, and justice.

Before January 1st of 1994, there were rapes of all kind. Not just of women, but of all humans. Being an indigenous person added a double silence to the fact of being a woman. Here, and I do not just refer to Chiapas but to the entire country, the human being is raped, dignity is raped, history is raped.

The indigenous Zapatista women, those women who do not belong to us but who march at our side, those women who are so far from the Peking Summit, those women who fight against everything and everyone (and this includes us Zapatista men), those Zapatista women, have decided to stop being women in order to win the right to be women. You know all this well. In the year or more that you have been our legal representative in the American Union, you have discovered us and have found thousands of those women (and men) who are your sisters and with whom you are united by something which is in your blood: human dignity.

The compañeras comandantes of the CCRI-CG of the EZLN will give you our communiqué in regards to this aggression which you have suffered, and that all of us Zapatistas suffer with you. They are the ones with the best ability for it. Personally, I feel incapable of putting to paper the bridge of support, sympathy, and admiration which you inspire in me. My clumsiness, or perhaps my fear of being clumsy, ties up my words. They, our compañeras, are not free because they are Zapatistas. But the fact that they are Zapatistas, as you are, makes them fighters who fight to change everything, including us. Rape is not solely the concern of women, it involves all men, not only because men are capable of its perpetration, but because we can be accomplices as well, by engaging in harmful ridicule and by our silence. But the struggle for respect for the specificity of gender, can also include us, by acknowledging what we are, what we are not, and above all, what we are capable of becoming.

So I do not write to you as though you were someone who sympathizes with Zapatismo and is wounded for that reason.

I write to you as a compañera, as a Zapatista. Perhaps this can explain the paucity of these thoughts and the hesitant lines which try to express it. I only write to you, in the name of my Zapatista compañeras and compañeros, to remind you and to remind all of us that we are one, we are the intuition that something new is possible, and that the fight in order to win it is worth it.

OK.

Salud, and with hope that humiliation not be the present or future of women, or of any human being.

From the mountains of the Mexican Southeast,
Subcomandante Insurgente Marcos.

THE TALE OF THE LIME WITH AN IDENTITY CRISIS
JANUARY 9, 1998

Once upon a time, there was a lime who was in torment.

"I'm neither a lemon nor an orange," it told itself, worrying a great deal as it hung from its tree. It looked and looked at the oranges on their tree and the lemons, too, and grew even more tormented because it didn't belong anyplace. Then Saul and Andulio came along, cut the lime down from its tree, and began playing soccer with it, using it for a ball.

"I'm cured!" shouted the ex-lime, as Andulio dribbled to Saul and kicked it toward the opposing goal, which was, of course, a chicken coop. The yell—G-o-o-o-o-a-l—woke up a little piglet who, thinking he was a chick, had been sleeping on a roost in the chicken coop.

Moral: The closet has more than one door.

LETTER TO MUMIA ABU-JAMAL
APRIL 24, 1999

To: Mumia Abu-Jamal
American Union

Mr. Mumia:

I am writing to you in the name of the men, women, children, and elderly of the Zapatista Army of National Liberation in order to congratulate you on April 24, which is your birthday.

Perhaps you have heard of us. We are Mexican, mostly indigenous communities, and we took up arms on January 1 of 1994 demanding a voice, face, and name for the forgotten of the earth.

Since then, the Mexican government has waged war on us, and pursues us, and harasses us seeking our death, our disappearance and our definitive silence. The reason? These lands are rich with oil, uranium and precious lumber. The government wants them for the great transnational companies. We want them for all the Mexicans. The government sees our lands as a business. We see our history written in these lands. In order to defend our right (and that of all Mexicans) to live with liberty, democracy, justice, and dignity, we became an army and undertook a name, voice, and face.

Perhaps you wonder how we know of you, about your birthday, and why it is that we extend this long bridge that goes from the mountains of the Mexican Southeast to the prison of Pennsylvania, which has imprisoned you unjustly. Many good people from many parts of the world have spoken of you, and through them we have learned how you were ambushed by the North American police in December of 1981, of the lies which they constructed in the procedures against you, and of the death sentence in 1982. We learned about your birthday through the international mobilizations which, under the name of "Millions for Mumia," are being prepared this April 24th.

It is harder to explain the bridge that this letter extends; it is more complicated. I could tell you that, for the powerful people of Mexico and the government, to be an indigenous person, or to look like an indigenous person, is reason for disdain, abhorrence, distrust, and hatred. The racism which now floods the palaces of Power in Mexico goes to the extreme of carrying out a war of extermination, genocide, against millions of indigenous people. I am sure that you will find similarities with what the Power in the United States does with the so-called "people of color" (African-American, Chicanos, Puerto Ricans, Asians, North-American Indians, and any other peoples who do not have the insipid color of money).

We are also "people of color" (the same color of our brothers who have Mexican blood and live and struggle in the American Union). We are of the color "brown," the color of the earth, the color from which we take our history, our strength, our wisdom, and our hope. But in order to struggle we add another color to the brown: black. We use black ski-masks to show our faces. Only in this way can we be seen and heard. We chose this color as a result of the counsel of an indigenous Mayan elder who explained to us what the color black meant.

The name of this wise elder was Old Man Antonio. He died in these rebel Zapatista lands in March of 1994, victim of tuberculosis which ate his lungs and his breath. Old Man Antonio used to tell us that from black came the light and from there came the stars which light up the sky around the world. He told us a story which said that a long time ago (in those times when no one measured it), the first gods were given the task of giving birth to the world. In one of their meetings they saw it was necessary that the world have life and movement, and for this light was necessary. Then they thought of making the sun in order that the days move and so there would be day and night and time for struggling and time for making love. The gods had their meeting and made this agreement in front of a large fire, and they knew it was necessary that one of them be sacrificed by throwing himself into the fire, in order to become fire himself, and fly into the sky. The gods thought that the work of the sun was the most important, so they chose the most beautiful god so that he would fly into the fire and become the sun. But he was afraid. Then the smallest god, the one who was black, said he was not afraid, and he threw himself into the fire and became sun. Then the world had light and movement, and there was time for struggle and time for love, and in the day the bodies worked to make the world, and in the night the bodies made love and sparkles filled the darkness.

This is what Old Man Antonio told us, and that is why we use a black ski mask. So we are of the color brown and of the color black. But we are also of the color yellow, because the first people who walked these lands were made of corn so that they would be true. And we are also red, because this is for the call of blood that has dignity; and we are also blue, because we are the sky in which we fly; and green, for the mountain that is our house and our strength. And we are white, because we are paper, so that tomorrow can write its story.

So, we are seven colors because there were seven first gods who birthed the world.

This is what Old Man Antonio said long ago, and now I tell you this story so that you may understand the reason for this bridge of paper and ink which I send to you all the way from the mountains of the Mexican Southeast.

And also so that you may understand that with this bridge goes pieces of salutes and hugs for Leonard Peltier (who is in the prison at Leavenworth, Kansas), and for the more than 100 political prisoners in the USA who are the victims of injustice, stupidity, and authoritarianism.

Along with this letter-bridge walks a salute to the Diné (the Navajo), who, in Big Mountain, Arizona, fight against the violations of their traditional Diné religious practices. They struggle against those who prefer the large businesses instead of respect for the religious freedom of Indian peoples, and those who want to destroy sacred grounds and ceremonial sites (as is the case of Peabody Western Coal Company which wants to take lands without reason, history, or rights—lands which belong to the Diné and their future generations.)

But there are not only stories of resistance against North American injustice in this letter-bridge. There are the indigenous peoples, from the extreme south of our continent, in Chile, the Mapuche women in the Pewenche Center of Alto Bio-Bio who resist against stupidity. Two indigenous women, Bertha and Nicolasa Quintreman, are accused of "mistreating" members of the armed forces of the Chilean government. So there it is. An armed military unit with rifles, sticks, and tear-gas, protected by bulletproof vests, helmets, and shields, accusing two indigenous women of "mistreatment." But Bertha is 74 years old, and Nicolasa is 60. How is it possible that two elderly people confronted a "heroic" group of heavily-armed military? Because they are Mapuche. The story is the same as that of the brothers and sisters Diné of Arizona, and the same which repeats itself in all America: a company (ENDESA) wants the lands of the Mapuches, and in spite of the law which protects the indigenous communities, the government is on the side of the companies. The Mapuche students have pointed out that the government and the company made a "study" of military intelligence about the indigenous Mapuche communities and they came to the conclusion that the Mapuche could not think, defend themselves, resist, or construct a better future. The study was wrong, apparently.

Now it occurs to me, that perhaps the powerful in North America carried out a "military intelligence" study (this is frankly a contradiction, because those of us who are military are not intelligent, if we were we would not be military) about the case of the Diné in Arizona, about Leonard Peltier, about other political prisoners, about yourself, Mister Mumia.

Perhaps they made this study and came to the conclusion that they might be able to violate justice and reason, to assault history and lose the truth. They thought they could do this and no one would say anything. The Diné Indians would stand by and watch the destruction of the most sacred of their history, Leonard Peltier would be alone, and you, Mister Mumia, would be silenced (and I remember your own words, "They not only want my death, they want my silence").

But the studies were wrong. Happy mistake? The Diné resist against those who would kill their memory, Leonard Peltier is accompanied by all of those who demand his liberty, and you sir, speak and yell today with all the voices that celebrate your birthday, as all birthdays should be celebrated, by struggling.

Mister Mumia:

We have nothing big to give you as a gift for your birthday; it is poor and little, but all of us send you an embrace.

We hope that when you gain your freedom you will come to visit us. Then we will give you a birthday party, even if it isn't April 24th, it will be an un-birthday party.

There will be musicians, dancing, and speaking, which are the means by which men and women of all colors understand and know one another, and build bridges over which they may walk together, towards history, towards tomorrow.

Happy Birthday!

OK. We salute you, and may justice and truth find their place.

From the mountains of the Mexican Southeast,
Subcomandante Insurgente Marcos.

P.S. I read somewhere that you are a father and a grandfather. So I am sending you a gift for your children and grandchildren. It is a little wooden car with Zapatistas dressed in black ski-masks.

Tell your children and grandchildren that it is a gift that we, the Zapatistas, send to you. Explain to them that there are people of all colors everywhere, just like you, who want justice, liberty, and democracy for people of all colors.

THE TRUE STORY OF MARY READ AND ANNE BONNY

So they lov'd, as love in twain,
Had the essence but in one,
Two distincts, division none,
Number there in love was slain.
—WILLIAM SHAKESPEARE
"THE PHOENIX AND THE TURTLE," II.25-28

For lesbians, homosexuals, transsexuals, and transvestites, with admiration
and respect.

While reviewing the parchments, I discovered a story that Durito is asking
me to include in his new book, Stories of Vigilance by Candlelight.
It is about a letter from an unknown sender (the signature is illegible).
The addressee is also an enigma; although it is clearly named, it is not
clear whether it is a he or a she. Better that you see it for yourselves. Upon
my soul, if the lack of definition between the masculine and feminine is
not quite explained in the epistle itself. The date is smudged, and we
don't have the technology here to verify when it was written. But it also
seems to me that it could have been as easily written centuries ago as
weeks ago. You'll know what I mean. OK, then.

Dear You:

Pirate stories tell of two women, Mary Read and Anne Bonny,
who disguised themselves as men and, as such, plowed through
the seas in the company of other buccaneers, taking towns and

vessels, hoisting the standard of the skull and crossbones. It was the year 1720 and different stories have one or the other living and fighting the rough seas of those times. On a pirate ship, commanded by Captain John Rackam, they met each other. The stories tell that love blossomed, one thinking the other was a man, but upon learning the truth, everything returned to normal, and they went their separate ways.

It wasn't like that. This letter I write to you is the true story of Mary Read and Anne Bonny. The letter trusts in this other story, the one that will not appear in books, because they still persist in spinning the normality and good sense that everything has, and the normality of the "other" goes no further than disapproving silence, condemnation, or neglect. This is part of the story that walks along the underground bridges that the "others" build, in order to be, and to be known.

The history of Mary Read and Anne Bonny is a history of love, and as such, it has its visible parts, but the greatest is always hidden, in the depths. In the visible part, there is a ship (a sloop, to be more precise), and a pirate, Captain John Rackam. Both ship and pirate were protectors and accomplices of that love that was so very "other" and "different" that the history from above had to cover it up for later generations.

Mary Read and Anne Bonny loved each other knowing they also shared the same essence. Some stories relate that the two were women, who, dressed as men, met each other knowing they were women and, as such, loved each other under the affectionate gaze of Lesbos. Others say that the two were men who hid behind pirates' clothes, and that they concealed their homosexual love and their passionate encounters behind the complicated story of women pirates disguised as men.

In either case, their bodies met in the mirror that discovers that which, for being so obvious, is forgotten; those corners of flesh that have knots that, when undone, inspire sighs and storms; places sometimes only those alike can know. With lips, skin, and hands, they built the bridges that joined those alike, making them different.

Yes, in whichever case, Mary Read and Anne Bonny were transvestites who, in the masquerade, discovered each other and met. In both cases, being the same, they revealed themselves to be different, and the two lost all divisions and became one. To the unconventionality of their being pirates, Mary Read and Anne Bonny added that to their "abnormal" and marvelous love.

Homosexuals or lesbians, transvestites always, Mary and Anne overcame with courage and boldness those whom "normality" would put in chains. While men surrendered without putting up any resistance, Mary and Anne fought to the end, before being taken prisoners.

Homosexuals or lesbians? I don't know, the truth was taken to the grave with John Rackam, when he was hanged in Port Royal, November 17, 1720; and to the shipwreck that cracked the sloop that served them as bed and accomplice. Whatever the case, their love was very "other" and great for being different. Because it happens that love follows its own paths and is, always, a transgressor of the law . . .

I do my duty by telling you this story.

Adiós.

(An illegible signature follows.)

There ends the story... or does it go on?

Durito says that those who are different in their sexual preferences are doubly "other" since they are "other" within those who are in themselves other.

I, a bit seasick from so much "other," ask him, "Can't you explain that a bit more?"

"Yes," says Durito. "When we are struggling to change things, we often forget that this includes changing ourselves."

Above, the dawn was about to change and make itself "other" and different. Rain followed, as well as struggle...

OK once more. *Salud*, and don't tell anyone, but I haven't been able to figure out how in the hell I'm going to fit into the sardine can (sigh).

El Sup, bailing water out of the frigate because, as you can imagine, it started to rain again and Durito says that bailing water is one of my "privileges"...

.

THE UN'S COMPLICITY IN THE WAR IN EUROPE WAS OBVIOUS

For Maurice Najman, who continues feigning death.

JULY 19, 1999

To: Asma Jahangir
UN Special Relator for Extrajudicial, Summary, and Arbitrary Executions

Madame Asma Jahangir:

I am writing to you in the name of the women, men, children, and elderly of the Zapatista Army of National Liberation.

We know that we will be receiving criticism for what I am going to say, and for having wasted a good opportunity to reveal the Mexican government in their genocidal policy against the Indian peoples. But, for us, "political opportunity" has little bearing in the face of political ethics. And it would not be ethical, given our confrontation with the Mexican government, for us to turn to an international body that has lost all credibility and legitimacy, and whose death certificate was signed with the NATO bombings in Kosovo.

With their war in the Balkans, the North American government—disguised as NATO, and with the regimes of England, Italy, and France as grotesque pawns—managed to destroy their primary objective: the United Nations (UN). The "intelligent" mega-police actions of the global gendarme, the US, made a fool of the once highest international forum. Violating the precepts that gave rise to the UN, NATO carried out a war of cynical aggression, attacked civilians indiscriminately, and tried to delegate intellectual authority to the satellites, who, more than ever, demonstrated that they are useless to those who already have the visions and who have made the decisions. NATO's bellicose cynicism was superseded only by the "brilliant" statements of their chiefs and spokespersons. The "humanitarian war," "the error in good faith," and the "collateral damage" were not the only pearls of war they were selling (because they were already counting on passing the bill) in Kosovar lands.

A NATO military person with a good number of stars on his chest made two statements in Brussels on Tuesday that caused chills: Out of a total of 35,000 air operations, more than 10,000 were directed at concrete targets. And the other 25,000? Could they have been carried out in error? If concrete targets exist, do non-concrete ones exist? What kind of target is a person? The second statement raised as many questions as the previous: NATO's objective was never to completely destroy the Yugoslav army, nor was it to reduce the country to ashes. Thank goodness, although one cannot help but think that, before ashes come embers, and before those, bits, and before those, pieces: to what size of material had they been thinking of reducing the country and its army? The postwar banquet is served, the news sent by Roger Waters' satellite fills the media all day long. When more is being said, that which cannot be said can be concealed all the better.
-Jordi Soler, in *La Jornada*, June 19, 1999

The UN's complicity in the war in Europe was obvious, and, given our position regarding this war, the minimum of consistency leads us to distance ourselves from an organization that for years, it is true, did indeed carry out a dignified and independent role in the international arena. It is not so today. On one side and the other of the planet, the UN has turned into a predictable legal support for the wars of aggression that the great power of money repeats, without becoming glutted of blood or of destruction.

But, if the UN's silence was the accomplice of crime and destruction in Kosovo, in Mexico it has taken a more active role in the war the Mexican government is carrying out against the indigenous peoples: in May 1998, at the request of the UNHCR [United Nations High Commissioner for Refugees], the government attacked the community of Amparo Aguatinta, beat up children, imprisoned men and women, and militarily occupied the seat, then, of the Tierra y Libertad Autonomous Municipality. The results of the UN's "humanitarian work" in Chiapas are in the Cerro Hueco Jail in Tuxtla Gutiérrez. More recently, today, July 19, 1999, Kofi Annan, the Secretary General of the UN, is delivering the United Nations Vienna Civil Society Prize to the self-styled Azteca Foundation. The Foundation, under the auspices of the native Milosevich, Ricardo Salinas Pliego, spends its time carrying out campaigns against drugs using cocaine addicts, promoting coup attempts, and destroying indigenous schools with helicopters. For that: for its ties with drug trafficking and for its calls for coups, the Azteca Foundation will receive a medal and a check for $25,000 from Mr. Annan.

And so we cannot have any confidence at all in the UN. And it is not out of chauvinism or in rejection of all things foreign. There have been—risking their lives, liberty, belongings, and prestige—men and women from the five continents, as international observers (we shall leave the term "foreigners" for those, like Zedillo and the members of his cabinet, who have no homeland other than money). To go no further back, the International Civil Commission for Human Rights Observation (CCIODH) was here in February of 1998. Not only are their initials larger than the UN's, so is their moral authority, their honesty, their commitment to the truth, and the authenticity of their struggle for a peace with justice and dignity. Men and women from Germany, Argentina, Canada, Denmark, France, Greece, Italy, Nicaragua, Switzerland, Andalusia, Aragon, Cantabria, Catalonia, the Basque Country, Galicia, Madrid, Murcia, and Alicante: all defied the Mexican government's most ferocious xenophobic campaign so far this century. They documented everything in a report (that they dedicated to the indigenous man Jose Tila López Garcia, assassinated after having presented his community's denunciations to the CCIODH). Consult this report; it is inspired not only by the desire for a dignified peace, but also by veracity and honesty.

After the CCIODH, another group of Italian observers came, also in 1998. Things were worse for them than for the CCIODH, because they were summarily expelled by the current aspirant for the Mexican presidency, Francisco Labastida, and by the person who is now in charge of international public relations for his campaign team, and who was responsible at that time for hundreds of illegal expulsions, Fernando Solis Cámara.

Thousands of men and women from all over the world have come here, all honorable and of good will, the majority of them young persons of the kind called "earinged," who bother the institutionalized left all over the world. They came here, and they saw what the government denies, a genocidal war. They left, many of them expelled, and they relayed, and they are relaying, what they saw: an unequal war between those who have all the military power (the government), and those who only have reason, history, truth, and tomorrow on their side (us). It is obvious who is going to win: we are.

And not just alone, international organizations as well, such as Amnesty International, Americas Watch, Global Exchange, Mexico Solidarity Network, the National Commission for Democracy in Mexico-USA, Pastors for Peace, Humanitarian Law Project, Doctors of the World, Bread for the World, Doctors without Borders, and many others whose names escape me now, but not their histories or their commitment to peace.

For us, any of them, individuals or groups, have more moral authority and more international legitimacy than the United Nations, converted today into a cocktail party for the end-of-century neoliberal wars.

With good reason the government representatives (the pathetic Ms. Green, the similar Rabasa, El Croquetas Albores, etcetera) say they have nothing to fear from your visit. They do not fear it because they know the UN has been an accomplice to, and, in the case of the Tierra y Libertad Autonomous Municipality, part of, the war of extermination against the Indian peoples of Mexico.

According to what we have read and heard, you are an honest person. You probably entered the service of the UN during the time when that organization was preventing wars, supporting different groups who were victims of government injustices, and promoting the development of the most needy. But now the UN promotes and supports wars, and it helps and awards those who are killing and humiliating the excluded of the world.

It has not escaped our attention that various international powers are nurturing the idea of using for their own benefit the rich oil and uranium deposits that exist under Zapatista soil. Those, up above, are making complicated accounts and calculations and entertaining the hope that the Zapatistas will make separatist proposals. It would be easier and cheaper to negotiate the purchase of the subsoil with the Banana Republic (Mayan Nation, they call it). After all, it is well known that indigenous people are satisfied with little mirrors and glass beads. Because of that, they are not giving up on their intent to involve themselves in the conflict and to manipulate it according to their interests. They have certainly not been able to, not on our side. Because it happens that the Zapatistas take "National Liberation," the names of the EZLN, very much to heart and sword. And, anachronistic as we are, we still believe in "outmoded" concepts, such as "national sovereignty" and "national independence." We have not accepted, nor will we accept, any foreign interference in our movement. We have not accepted, nor will we accept, any international force being a part of the conflict. We will fight it with the same or more decisiveness that we have fought against those who decreed death through forgetting for 10 million Mexican indigenous people. Those with moral authority and legitimacy will be welcomed, those who are not appendages of armed forces (such as NATO), or who have military forces at their service (such as the unhappily celebrated Blue Helmets of the UN), those who want to be part of the PEACEFUL solution of the conflict.

We do not need any help to make war; we can manage on our own. For peace, many are needed, but honest ones, and there are not many of those.

Do not be very unhappy, the UN is not the only official international body that collaborates with the Mexican government's counterinsurgency campaign. There you have the International Committee of the Red Cross, whose delegation in San Cristobal bordered on the sublime when speaking of servility and stupidity. At a meeting with displaced peoples from Polhó, the CICR delegates stated, without even blushing, that the displaced are not in their homes because they are lazy and because they want to be supported by the Red Cross. To those imbeciles, who wander around under the CICR's purported flags of neutrality and humanitarian aid, the paramilitaries are an invention, the product of the collective hysteria of more than 7,000 displaced indigenous men and women; the 45 executed at Acteal in reality died of infections, and peace and tranquility reign in Los Altos of Chiapas. One can assume that Albores has already congratulated them (and has offered them some of his bones, because he is not very into sharing we are told), and they are continuing to go about in their modern vehicles, fattening the curriculum vitae of that "distinguished" institution. How about that? The CICR will surely be the next to receive an award from the UN in their "civil society" competitions.

This dawn in which I am writing these lines, the moon is a scythe of cold light. It is the hour of the dead, of our dead. And you should know that the Zapatista dead are very restless and talkative. They still speak, despite the fact that they are dead, and they are shouting history. They are shouting it so that it does not sleep, so that memory does not die, so that our dead will live shouting...

Ocosingo, the 3rd and 4th of January, 1994. Federal Army troops take the municipal seat of Ocosingo—in Zapatista hands since the dawn of January 1—by assault. Following orders from the then Brigadier General Luis Humberto Portillo Leal—who had been chief of the 30th Military Zone—Infantry major Adalberto Perez Nava executed five members of the EZLN. General Portillo Leal had ordered the execution of the Zapatistas, whether or not they were armed. The instructions were to take no prisoners, all of them should be dead (they should only avoid killing them if the press were present, because that would damage the Army's image). The Second Infantry Captain, Lodegario Salvador Estrada, executed other Zapatista indigenous people. Days later, in the offices of the Department of National Defense, an Infantry Second Lieutenant, Jimenez Morales, was executed by military personnel in order to have him take the blame for the assassination of eight indigenous people in the IMSS hospital in Ocosingo. We did not invent any of this information, you can corroborate it in the act by the Department of Justice of the United States, Executive Office for Immigration Review, Immigration Court of El Paso, Texas, signed by Bertha A. Zuniga, Immigration Judge of the United States, dated March 19, 1999. Case Jesus Valles Bahena, A76-804-703. In this file, the officer Jesus Valles Bahena narrates why he had to desert from the Army, after having been threatened with death by Colonel Bocarundo Benavidez for his refusal to carry out orders for summary executions. Along with Valles, other officers refused to carry out instructions for assassination. Their fate is unknown.

These, Madame Jahangir, are the names, civilian and fighting, of those executed in Ocosingo, Chiapas on January 3 and 4 of 1994:

Comandante Hugo, Francisco Gómez Hernández.
Second Lieutenant Insurgente for War Materiel Alvaro, Silverio Gómez Alvarez.
Insurgente for War Materiel Fredy, Bartolo Pérez Cortes.

Infantry Insurgente Calixto, (civilian name cannot be revealed).
Infantry Insurgente Miguel, Arturo Aguilar Jiménez.
Miliciano Salvador, Eusebio Jiménez González.
Miliciano Ernesto, Santiago Pérez Montes.
Miliciano Venancio, Marcos Pérez Cordoba.
Miliciano Amador, Antonio Guzman González.
Miliciano Agenor, Fernando Ruíz Guzman.
Miliciano Fidelino, Marcos Guzman Pérez.
Miliciano Adan, Doroteo Ruíz Hernández.
Miliciano Arnulfo, Diego Aguilar Hernández.
Miliciano Samuel, Eliseo Hernández Cruz.
Miliciano Horacio, Juan Mendoza Lorenzo.
Miliciano Jeremias, Eliseo Sanchez Hernández.
Miliciano Linares, Leonardo Mendez Sanchez.
Miliciano Dionisio, Carmelo Mendez Mendez.
Miliciano Bonifacio, Javier Hernández López.
Miliciano Heriberto, Filiberto López Pérez.
Miliciano Jeremias, Pedro López Garcia.
Miliciano German, Alfredo Sanchez Pérez.
Miliciano Feliciano, Enrique González Garcia.
Miliciano Horacio, Manuel Sanchez González.
Miliciano Cayetano, Marcelo Pérez Jiménez.
Miliciano Cristobal, Nicolas Cortes Hernández.
Miliciano Chuchin, Vicente López Hernández.
Miliciano Adan, Javier López Hernández.
Miliciano Anastacio, Alejandro Santis López.

During those days, there were more who died, but they fell in combat, and were not executed.

In addition to execution, there was brazen torture, in Morelia, then the municipality of Altamirano. On January 7, 1994, the Army entered the community and kidnapped Severiano Santíz Gomez (60 years old), Hermelindo Santíz Gómez (65 years old), and Sebastian López Santíz (45 years old). A little later, their remains—with signs of fractures and with clear evidence of having been executed—were found. The analyses of the remains were carried out by specialists from the Physicians for Human Rights NGO.

Torture and execution were the methods also used by the "glorious" federal Army in the municipal seat of Las Margaritas, Chiapas. There, during the first days of combat, Major Teran (who had been previously tied to drug trafficking in the region) kidnapped, tortured, and executed Eduardo Gómez Hernández and Jorge Mariano Solis López in the neighborhood of Plan de Agua Prieta. Those executed had their ears and tongues cut off.

These deaths, our deaths, do not find rest. The butchers of Ocosingo and the assassins and torturers of Morelia and Las Margaritas continue to be free and to enjoy health and prosperity. Thousands of shadows are pursuing them now, and they are competing for the honor of seeing justice done.

Last year, contrary to what their propaganda for international consumption says, the government renewed its armed clashes with Zapatista forces. On June 10, 1998, a military column, heavy with infantry, tanks, planes, and helicopters, attacked the community of Chavajeval, in the municipality of San Juan de la Libertad (to the Zapatistas) or El Bosque (to the government). The Zapatista troops repelled the attack, and a heavy exchange of fire began, broadcast by a national television channel. Our troops brought down a helicopter, and, frustrated and angry, the soldiers retreated; but they attacked the community of Union Progreso that same day of June 10, 1998. There they took seven Zapatista militia prisoners and summarily executed them. These are their names:

Miliciano Enrique, Adolfo Gómez Díaz.
Miliciano Jeremias, Bartolo López Mendez.
Miliciano Jorge, Lorenzo López Mendez.
Miliciano Marcelino, Andres Gómez Gómez
Miliciano Gilberto, Antonio Gómez Gómez.
Miliciano Alfredo, Sebastian Gómez Gómez.
Miliciano Pedro, Mario Sanchez Ruíz.

(The television reporter who covered the military attack on Chavajeval received the national journalism prize. Over indigenous and rebel blood, his employers rewarded him, sending him to cover the campaign of one of the two intellectual assassins of *Union Progreso*—the other is Zedillo—the then Secretary of Government and now presidential aspirant, Francisco Labastida Ochoa).

This is the Mexican federal Army, the one that now wants to present an innocent image, announcing the dispatch of almost 7,000 more troops to the Selva Lacandona, with the story that they are going to plant little trees. Everyone is silent. The military chief says that the 7,000 are going unarmed, and the 7,000 arrive armed. Everyone is silent.

This is the "new" government strategy that has been promised you by the pathetic character named Rabasa Gamboa (who is paid, and paid well, for coordinating emptiness). And since we are on this subject, a new bray by Rabasa clarifies that Acteal was not an execution.

This time he is right: Acteal, and all the policies followed by his boss Ernesto Zedillo, is GENOCIDE.

This is the history. With Ernesto Zedillo's gaining of power— through assassination—the federal Army gained cover and money in order to bring up their longing for blood and death.

Seeking to improve the Army's depleted public image, paramili- tary squadrons were activated, organized by active duty soldiers, trained by soldiers, equipped by soldiers, protected by soldiers, directed by soldiers, and, in not a few cases, created by soldiers, as well as by Institutional Revolutionary Party members. The objec- tive was, and is, clear; it was, and is, about turning the conflict around and presenting it to the international public (the national public does not even minimally matter to them) as an inter-ethnic war, or, as the corrupt PGR tries to present it, as an inter-family war. The names chosen by the soldiers to baptize their new paramilitary units reflect their great imagination: Red Mask (their greatest "military" success: the Acteal massacre). Peace and Justice (responsible for the assassinations of dozens of indigenous people in the north of the state). Chinchulines (they act in the North and in the Selva). Anti-Zapatista Indigenous Revolutionary Movement (they have training camps in military barracks in the Cañadas, and are financed by the state PRI delegation). Los Puñales (they are active in Comitán and Las Margaritas). Albores of Chiapas (they are directly dependent on El Croquetas Albores Guillen, they wear green caps and their war cry is "Albores carries through!")

The "new" government strategy for Chiapas is in plain view: in the ejido of El Portal, in Frontera Comalapa, a group of Zapatista families demand that water service be restored, service which was taken away from them by PRI soldiers in complicity with the municipal president there. Zapatista indigenous people demanding anything is something the government cannot tolerate, given that, for them, the only thing the Zapatistas should be receiving is blows and bullets. In response to the Zapatista civil demonstration, the government mobilized the police. The PRI, emboldened by the presence of the police, charged the Zapatistas with sticks and shots; two Zapatistas are seriously wounded. The police act rapidly and detain the Zapatistas, accusing them of criminal association for having been found with ski-masks. With the alacrity afforded by the "State of Law" in Chiapas, a state government helicopter transfers the prisoners, in order to be tried "for breaching the peace" (because, in Chiapas, demanding potable water is an attack against the peace). The two wounded are fighting for their lives in the hospital, those who fired are free and healthy, and, in Government Palace, the new "victory" is being celebrated in the war against the EZLN. You will see none of this in the written or electronic press, too concerned with giving the front pages to Albores' barking dogs or to the PRI aspirants' fair of hypocrisy and fallacies. Zapatista indigenous soldiers imprisoned, beaten, wounded, or assassinated are no longer news in Mexico. They are part of daily life.

This is the "new" federal government strategy for Chiapas, of Zedillo's government. There is nothing new about it, nor is it a strategy, it is the same stupid pounding that assumes that those who have known how to resist for 500 years will not be able to do so for a year and a half.

Concerning Ernesto Zedillo Ponce de León, one must say now what everyone will be saying tomorrow: he is a man of no word, a liar and an assassin. This is what we are saying today. When he leaves Los Pinos, everyone (even those who are treating him with respect today) will be repeating it, and all of his corruption and crimes will come to public light. Persecution, exile, jail: these are the probable stations for his future. It does not make us unhappy; our dead do not make us unhappy.

I read in the press that you have had meetings with some Non-governmental Organizations in Mexico City, and you will have others during your visit to Chiapas, these days. I congratulate you, may you have the good fortune and the honor to personally know men and women who—without official and/or institutional paraphernalia—have confronted every kind of threat and persecution for their work in defense of human rights in Mexico.

I will not put any names here, because, in Mexico, and especially in Chiapas, the NGOs that are fighting for human rights are military objectives for the federal Army. But any of these NGO's, whether the smallest or the most newly created, have more moral authority in the Mexico of below than the UN does. Regardless, perhaps you are not to blame, and it is only the great leaders of the UN who have accepted, without even protesting, the sporadic role of spokespersons for NATO, and being accomplices in the Mexican government's war of extermination against the Indian peoples.

Nonetheless, we are not pessimists regarding the future of the international community. The UN's failure is not humanity's failure. A new international order is possible, a better one, more just, more human. In it, there will have to be a dominant place for all those international and national NGOs (who, unlike the UN, do not have at their service—or are at the service of—military forces), and for all those men, women, children, and old ones who understand that the future of the world is being debated between the exclusionary difference (the war in Kosovo) and the world where many worlds fit (of which Zapatismo in Chiapas is, almost, a suggestion).

With them, and especially for them, the world will someday be a place where war will be a disgrace and peace a reality, and the relators for the various human rights violations, specimens whose only arena of action will be researching the pre-history of humanity.

Excuse the tone, Madame Asma Jahangir, it is not that this is a personal matter against you, it is just that the organization you represent no longer represents anything. That, and also that we do not forget Kosovo, nor Amparo Aguatinta, nor Ocosingo, nor Morelia, nor Las Margaritas, nor *Unión Progreso,* nor anything. Whatever happens, we do not forget.

We do not forget.

OK.
Salud, and may dignity never forget memory. If it were to lose it, it would die.

From the mountains of the Mexican Southeast,
Subcomandante Insurgente Marcos.

FIFTEEN YEARS AGO
SEPTEMBER, 1999

For Rodolfo Peña
Another mistaken embrace by death

Every August, year after year, the mountains of the Mexican southeast arrange themselves so as to give birth to a particularly luminous dawn. I know nothing of the scientific causes, but during this dawn, a single one throughout the disconcerting August, the moon is a hammock of swaying iridescence, the stars arrange themselves so as to be background and object, and the Milky Way proudly illuminates its thousand wounds of clotted light. This August at the end of the millennium, the calendar was announcing the sixth day when this dawn appeared. And so, with the swaying moon, the memory returned of another August 6th, when, 15 years ago, I began my entrance into these mountains that were and are, without wanting it or willing it, house, school, road, and door. I began to enter in August and I did not finish doing so until September.

I should confess something to you: when I laboriously climbed the first of the steep hills that abound in these lands, I felt that it would be the last. I was not thinking of revolution, of the high ideals of humans, or of a shining future for the dispossessed and forgotten.

No, I was thinking that I had made the worst decision of my life, that the pain that was increasingly squeezing my chest would end up definitively closing off the ever more skimpy entrance of air, that the best thing would be for me to return and to let the revolution arrange itself without me, along with other similar ruminations. If I did not go back, it was simply because I did not know the path of return, and I only knew that I should follow the compañero who preceded me, and who—to judge by the cigarette he was smoking while crossing the mud without difficulty—seemed to be merely out for a stroll. I did not think that one day I would be able to climb a hill smoking and not feeling that I was dying with each step, nor that a time would come when I would be able to negotiate the mud that abounded below as much as the stars did above. No, I was not thinking then; I was concentrating on every breath I was trying to take.

Finally, what happened is that at some point we reached the highest point of the hill, and the one who was in charge of the meager column (we were three) said that we would rest there. I let myself fall into the mud that appeared the closest, and I told myself that perhaps it would not be so difficult to find the return path, and that someday I would reach the point where the truck had dropped us off. I was making my calculations, including the excuses I would give, and that I would give to myself, for having abandoned the beginning of my career as a guerrilla fighter, when the compañero approached me and offered me a cigarette. I refused with a shake of my head, not because I didn't want to talk, but because I had tried to say "no thanks," but only a groan came out.

After a bit, taking advantage of the fact that the person in charge had retired some distance away, in order to satisfy biological needs referred to as "basic," I got up as best as I could above the 20-caliber shotgun I was carrying, more as a walking stick than as a combat weapon. In that way, I could see from the top of that mountain something which had a profound impact on me.

No, I did not look down, not towards the twisted scribble of the river, nor at the weak lights of the bonfires that were dimly illuminating a distant hamlet, nor at the neighboring mountains that painted the cañada, sprinkled with small villages, fields, and pastures.

I looked upwards. I saw a sky that was gift and relief—no, more of a promise. The moon was like a smiling nocturnal hammock, the stars sprinkling blue lights and the ancient serpent of luminous wounds that you call the "Milky Way," seemed to be resting its head there, very far away.

I remained looking for a time, knowing I would have to climb up that wretched hill in order to see this dawn, that the mud, the slips, the stones that hurt the skin on the outside and the inside, the tired lungs, incapable of pulling in the necessary air, the cramped legs, the anguished clinging to the shotgun-walking stick in order to free my boots from the prison of mud, the feeling of aloneness and desolation, the weight I was carrying on my back, is what had made it possible for that moon, those stars, and that Milky Way to be there and in no other place.

When I heard behind me the orders to renew the march, up in the sky a star, certainly fed up with being subjugated by the black roof, managed to break away, and, falling, left on the nocturnal blackboard a brief and fugitive tracing. "That's what we are," I said to myself. "Fallen stars that barely scratched the sky of history with a scrawl." As far as I knew, I had only thought this, but it seems I had thought it out loud, because the compañero asked: "What did he say?" "I don't know," replied the one in charge. "It could be he's already come down with a fever. We have to hurry."

This that I am recounting to you happened 15 years ago. Thirty years ago, some scribbled history, and, knowing it, they began calling to many others so that, by force of scribbles, scratches, and scrawls, they would end up breaking the veil of history, and the light would finally be seen; that, and nothing else, is the struggle we are making. And so if you ask us what we want, we will unashamedly respond: "To open up a crack in history."

Perhaps you are asking what happened to my intentions of returning and of abandoning the guerrilla life, and you might suppose that the vision of that first dawn in the mountain had made me abandon my ideas of fleeing, had lifted my morale and solidified my revolutionary consciousness. You are wrong. I put my plan into operation and went down into the mud. What happened is that I made a mistake, and went down the wrong side. Instead of going down the slope that would take me back to the road, and from there to "civilization," I went down the side that took me deeper into the jungle and that led me to another hill, and to another, and to another.

That was 15 years ago. Since then I have continued climbing hills and I have continued making the mistake about which side to go down. August continues birthing a special dawn every 6th, and all of us continue to be fallen stars, barely scratching history.

Vale de nuez, salud, and one minute! Wait. What is that shining brightly in the distance? It looks like a crack...

The Sup, on top of the hill,
tossing a coin in order to see which side of the hill leads down.

LETTER TO LEONARD PELTIER
OCTOBER, 1999

Leonard:

Through NCDM and Cecilia Rodriguez, we extend greetings from the men, women, children, and elders of the Zapatista Army of National Liberation.

Cecilia has told us about the grave injustice the North American judicial system has committed against you. We understand that the powerful are punishing your spirit of rebellion and your strong fight for the rights of indigenous people in North America.

Stupid as it is, the powerful believe that through humiliation, arrogance, and isolation, they can break the dignity of those who give thoughts, feelings, life, and guidance to the struggle for recognition and respect for the first inhabitants of the land, over whom the vain United States has risen. The heroic resistance that you have maintained in prison, as well as the broad movement of solidarity that your case and your cause have motivated in the United States and the world, reveal their mistake.

Knowing of your existence and history, no woman or man (if they are honest and conscious) can remain silent before such a great injustice. Nor can they remain still in front of a struggle which, like all that is born and grows from below, is necessary, possible, and true.

The Lakota, a people who have the honor and fortune to have you among their blood, have an ethic that recognizes and respects the place of all people and things, respects the relations that mother earth has with herself and other living things that live and die within her and outside of her. An ethic that recognizes generosity as a measure of human worth, the walk of our ancestors and our dead along the paths of today and tomorrow, women and men as part of the universe that have the power of free will to choose paths and seasons, the search for harmony and the struggle against that which breaks and disorders it. All of this, and more that escapes because we are so far away, has a lot to teach the "Western" culture which steers, in North America and in the rest of the world, against humanity and against nature.

Probably the determined resistance of Leonard Peltier is incomprehensible to the powerful in North America, and the world. To never give up, to resist. The powerful call this "foolishness."

But the foolish are in every corner of the world, and in all of them, resistance flourishes in the fertile ground of the most ancient history.

In sum, what the powerful fail to understand is not only Peltier's resistance, but also the entire world, and so they intend to mold the planet into the coffin the system represents: with wars, jails, and police officers.

Probably, the powerful in North America think that in jailing and torturing Leonard Peltier, they are jailing and torturing one man.

And so they don't understand how a prisoner can continue to be free, while in prison.

And they don't understand how, being imprisoned, he speaks with so many, and so many listen.

And they don't understand how, in trying to kill him, they give him more life.

And they don't understand how one man, alone, is able to resist so much, to represent so much, to be so large.

"Why?" the powerful ask themselves, and the answer never reaches their ears: Because Leonard Peltier is a people, the Lakota, and it is impossible to keep a people imprisoned.

Because Leonard Peltier speaks through the Lakota men and women who are, in themselves and in their nature, the best of mother earth.

Because the strength that this man and this people have does not come from modern weapons; rather it comes from their history, their roots, their dead.

Because the Lakota know that no one is more alive than the dead.

Because the Lakota, and many other North American Indian people, know that resisting without surrender not only defends their lives and their liberty, but also their history and the nature that gives them origin, home, and destiny.

Because the great ones always seem so small to those who cannot see the history that each one keeps inside.

Because the racism that now governs can only imagine the other, and the different, in jail or in the trashcan, where two Lakota natives were found last month, murdered, in the community of Pine Ridge. This is justice in North America: those who fight for their people are in jail, those who despise and murder walk unpunished.

What is Leonard Peltier accused of?

Not of a crime he didn't commit. No. He is accused of being other, of being different, of being proud to be other and different.

But for the powerful, Leonard Peltier's most serious "crime" is that he seeks rescue in the past, in his culture, in his roots, the history of his people, the Lakota. And for the powerful, this is a crime, because knowing oneself with history impedes one from being tossed around by this absurd machine that is the system.

If Leonard Peltier is guilty, then we are all guilty because we seek out history, and on its shoulders we fight to have a place in the world, a place of dignity and respect, a place for ourselves exactly as we are, which is also very much as we were.

If the Indian people of the North and Indian people of Mexico, as well as the indigenous people of the entire continent, know that we have our own place (being who we are, not pretending to be another skin color, another tongue, another culture), what is left is for the other colors that populate the entire world to know it. And what is left is for the powerful to know it. So that they know it, and learn the lesson so well that they won't forget—many more paths and bridges are needed that are walked from below.

On these paths and bridges, you, Leonard Peltier, have a special place, the best, next to us who are like you.

Salud, Leonard Peltier, receive a hug from one who admires and respects you, and who hopes that one day you will call him "brother."

OK, *salud*, and I hope that injustice disappears tomorrow, with yesterday as a weapon and today as a road.

From the mountains of the Mexican Southeast,
Subcomandante Insurgente Marcos

WHY WE USE THE WEAPON OF RESISTANCE
OCTOBER 26, 1999

I would like to thank those who were in charge of the Alicia Multiforum for the invitation they extended to us to participate in this roundtable.

I do not have much experience in round tables; square tables are more our specialty, as the table most certainly must be where those who are accompanying this act are seated: Zack de la Rocha, Yaotl, Hermann Bellinghausen, Nacho Pineda, a *compa* from the Punk Anarchy collective, and Javier Elorriaga.

What's more, it is quite likely that the participants at this roundtable that is not round are seated on a small platform. Furthermore, perhaps there is not even a table, but only a few chairs. Perhaps the only one who has a table is me, because they have to put the TV on something in order to show you this video.

Good. The fact is, at this round table, those who are participating cannot see each other's faces, something that would most certainly be happening if they were at a round table that was, in fact, round. And so here we are, sitting around a round table that is not round, and facing you, which is better, because from here I'm able to see a guy whose face is the best argument for leaving the issue of round and square tables in peace, and better that I don't tell you what that look is suggesting either (sigh).

Where was I? Oh, yes! Here we are, facing you, at that round table that I don't know, titled "From Underground Culture to the Culture of Resistance." No, I don't have anything against whoever called this round table, that isn't round, that. The problem is the repetition of that word: "CULTURE." So many things fit there that, even though we are restricting them to the limits imposed by the words "Underground" and "Resistance," they would not do for a round table, no matter how square it might be, but rather for a great intercontinental encounter that would last for eons, without even including the time taken up in arranging the microphone, greeting the raza, or in staying asleep because someone has decided that culture can also be boring and has set about demonstrating it.

Having said that, I am not going to talk to you about underground culture, nor about the culture of resistance, nor about the bridge that most certainly joins them. In addition to leaving these issues for those who are accompanying us at that table—that we are calling round even knowing that it is square—I will avoid making myself appear ridiculous and I will be able to conceal my encyclopedic ignorance on this subject. As the greatest and well-loved Don Durito of La Lacandona would say, "There is no problem sufficiently great that you can't get around it." I would add to those wise words that cause the action and the commitment, "nor is there a round table that is not square."

I know that you are all anxious to know what in the hell I'm going to talk about then. More than one of you might be asking if the guitar I have by my side means that I'm going to play a song, one of those that are so honorably played in the Mexico of below, which we all are.

But no, I'm not going to play any songs. The guitar is for the surprise appearance we're going to make tomorrow, October 27, 1999, with Rage Against the Machine, Aztlán Underground, and Tijuana NO at the Sports Palace. Well, that's if they don't censor us first, or if the law doesn't show up, in which case the concert will be held in the prison closest to your hearts.

And, I'm going to be sincere with you; this entire initial litany has been to use up time, because the organizers made it quite clear to me that I was to speak for some 20 minutes, and I believe that 20 minutes is too long to say that I'm not going to speak to you about underground culture, nor about the culture of resistance, nor about the relationship between the one and the other.

You know? We are warriors. We are warriors who are very "other," but warriors nonetheless. And we warriors know a few things. And among the few things that we know, we know about weapons.

So, better that I talk to you about weapons. Specifically, I'm going to talk to you about the weapon of resistance.

We, besides being warriors, are indigenous Mexicans. We live in the mountains of the Mexican Southeast, which is turning out to be the most distant corner of this country. We live like the majority of the indigenous people in Mexico live, that is, very badly.

Our homes have dirt floors, our walls are made from sticks or mud, and our roofs are tin, cardboard, or grass. A single room serves as kitchen, dining room, bedroom, living room, and chicken coop. Basically, our foods are maize, beans, chili, and the vegetables that grow in the field. For medicine we have a popular pharmacy, small and poorly stocked. Doctors? In our dreams. The school, if it is not being occupied by the government's soldiers, is a hall where up to four different groups of students gather at the same time. They are not very numerous, because our children start working when they're very small, between four and five years old, the girls carrying wood, grinding maize, washing clothes, and taking care of their younger brothers and sisters; between the ages of ten and twelve, the boys go to the mountain, taking care of the livestock, carrying wood, working the fields, the coffee plantations, or the pasture. Our lands are poor in two senses: they are poor because they belong to us, who are poor as a matter of course; and they are poor because they yield little in the way of harvest. We have only mud and rocks. The ranchers have the good lands. The livestock and coffee that we sell to make money, we sell to the *coyotes*, middlemen who pay us up to ten times less than the price of our products in the market. And so, our work, in addition to being hard, is badly paid.

However, even though we live like most of the indigenous population in the country, that is, in poverty, our lives are not the same. Our poverty is the same as the poverty of the others, but it is different; it is an "other" poverty. We are poor because that is what we have chosen. From the beginning of our uprising, they have offered us everything to get us to sell ourselves—to surrender.

If we had done so, if we had surrendered, if we had sold ourselves, we would now have good houses, good schools, hospitals, machinery for working the land, better prices for our products, good food.

We chose not to sell ourselves, we chose not to surrender. Because it so happens that we are indigenous and we are also warriors. And warriors are warriors because they are fighting for something. And we, the Zapatistas, are fighting for good homes, good food, good health, a good price for our work, good lands, good education, respect for the culture, the right to information, liberty, independence, justice, democracy, and peace. Yes, we are fighting for all of that, but for everyone, not just for ourselves. That is why we Zapatistas are warriors, because we want "For everyone, everything; nothing for ourselves."

If we had surrendered, if we had sold ourselves, we would no longer have been poor, but others would have continued to be so.

Good. But you are asking yourselves: Where is the weapon that this handsome, attractive, nice warrior was going to talk to us about? I'll tell you now.

It happened that, when they saw that we were not surrendering, that we were not selling ourselves, the government began attacking us in order to force us to surrender and to sell ourselves. They offered us many things—money, projects, aid—and when we rejected them, they became angry and threatened us. That is how we came to understand that, by refusing to accept government aid—by resisting—we made the powerful angry; and there is nothing a Zapatista warrior likes more than making the powerful angry. So with singular joy we dedicated ourselves to resisting, to saying "no," to transforming our poverty into a weapon—the weapon of resistance.

Almost six years of war have now spoken with that weapon; with it we have resisted more than 60,000 soldiers, war tanks, bomber aircraft, artillery helicopters, cannons, machine guns, bullets, and grenades. With it, we have resisted the lie.

If you would like me to sum it up, I will tell you that though we made ourselves soldiers so that one day soldiers would no longer be necessary, we also remain poor, so that one day there will no longer be poverty. For this we use the weapon of resistance.

Obviously, it is not the only weapon we have, as is clear from the metal that clothes us. We have other arms. For example, we have the arm of the word. We also have the weapon of our culture, of being what we are. We have the weapon of music, the weapon of dance. We have the weapon of the mountain, that old friend and compañera who fights along with us, with her roads, hiding places, and hillsides, with her trees, with her rains, with her suns, with her dawns, with her moons...

We also have the weapons that we carry by nature, but it is not the time to be going around punning, much less now, when you've all become very serious. And in order to chase away your seriousness, I'm going to tell you a joke—no, don't believe it or be frightened. I'm not going to tell you a joke; better that we leave that to Zedillo, who, as president, is nothing but a bad joke. No, better that I go on to the next issue that I'm going to talk to you about.

...It is not just the Zapatistas who are warriors of resistance. There are many groups (and there are several gathered together here) who have also made a weapon of resistance, and they are using it. There are indigenous peoples, there are workers, there are women, there are homosexuals, there are lesbians, there are students, there are young people. Above all there are young people, men and women, who name their own identities: "punk," "ska," "goth," "metal," "trasher," "rapper," "hip-hopper," and "etceteras." If we look at what they all have in common, we will see that they have nothing in common, that they are all "different." They are "others." And that is exactly what we have in common, that we are "other," and "different." Not only that, we also have in common that we are fighting in order to continue being "other" and "different," and that is why we are resisting. And to those in power, we are "other" and "different." We are not like they want us to be, but what we are.

And what we are—far from wanting to impose its being on the "other" or "different"—seeks its own space, and, at the same time, a space of meeting. The "punks" don't go around on a campaign demanding that all young people be "punks," nor do the "ska," or the "goths," or the "metal heads," or the "trashers," or the "rappers," or, certainly, the indigenous people. Nonetheless, Power does indeed want us to be how they want us to be, to dress according to the style it dictates, to talk the way it says, to eat what it sells, to consider beautiful and lovely what it considers beautiful and lovely. Power even wants us to love and hate the way it establishes that love and hate should be. And not just that, Power also wants us to do all this on our knees and in silence, without going around jumping, without shouts, without the uprisings of indigenous communities, all well-mannered. That is why Power has armies and police, to force those who are "other" and "different" to be the same, identical.

But the "other" and "different" are not looking for everyone to be like them. It is as if each one is saying, "Everyone has his own way or her own thing" (I don't know how that's said these days). And in order for this to be possible, it is not enough to just be; you must be while respecting the other. "Everyone doing his own thing" is double: it is affirmation of difference, and it is respect for the other difference. When we say we are fighting for respect for our "different" and "other" selves, that includes fighting for respect for those who are also "other" and "different," who are not like ourselves. And it is here where this entire resistance movement—called "underground" or "subterranean," because it takes place among those below and underneath institutional movements—meets Zapatismo.

And this meeting is a meeting between warriors, among those who make resistance a weapon, and who fight with it in order to be what they are, in order to exist.

Or, when Zapatistas say, "we want a world where many worlds fit," they are not discovering anything new, they are simply saying what the "other" and "different" who walk the worlds of below have already said.

We Zapatistas say, "I am as I am and you are as you are. Let's build a world where I can be, without having to cease being me, where you can be, without having to cease being you, and where neither I nor you force another to be like me or like you." So when the Zapatistas say, "a world where many worlds fit," they are saying, more or less, "Everyone does their own thing."

It so happens then that because we are different, we are the same. We are the same persecuted, the same despised, the same beaten, the same imprisoned, the same disappeared, the same assassinated. And it is not our people who are persecuting, despising, beating, imprisoning, assassinating us. It is not even the "others" from below. It is the Power and its names. And our crimes are not stealing, beating, assassinating, insulting. Nor is our crime being "other" and "different." No, our crime is in being who we are, and being proud of being so. Our crime—which, in Power's penal code, merits the death penalty—is the struggle we are making to continue being "other" and "different." If we were "other" and "different" shamefully, in hiding, guiltily, betrayed by ourselves, trying to be, or to appear to be, what Power wants us to be or to appear to be, then they would give us an indulgent and pitying little pat, and say to us: "These things happen when you are young; you will get over it with age." For Power, the medicine against rebellion is time, since "it will go away with age."

But what Power is not saying is what is behind that "age," what it assumes will cure and do away with youthful rebellion. Hours, months, and years of blows, insults, jails, deaths, rapes, persecutions, and neglect. A machinery working to "cure us" if we stop being what we are and if we turn ourselves into servile beings. A machinery that will eliminate us if we insist on being who we are, without regard to calendar, birthdays, or the date on our birth certificate.

And so, we are all transgressors of the law. Because there is a law in this system that kills and silences those who are "other" and "different." And, by living, by shouting—by talking, that is, by being rebels—we are transgressing that law, and we are, automatically, criminals.

And these criminals that we are—we live in a rebel reality, where resistance is a bridge that allows us to meet, recognizing our difference and our equality. Rock music is also like a bridge over which these realities walk in order to meet.

In what way is "rock" a mirror and crystal for this very "other" and "different" reality? The truth is, I don't know, and I don't understand. I look at and listen to groups like Rage Against the Machine and Tijuana NO (to mention just those who are participating in tomorrow's concert, but knowing that there are many others, and that all of them are good musicians and good human beings), and I ask myself why do they do what they do, say what they say, and play what they play? I believe it would be better for them to tell us what goes on with them. Perhaps it so happens that they are also asking themselves why we Zapatistas do what we do, say what we say, and play what we are playing (although, when it comes to rock, we are fairly useless. "Useless." How about that? A good name for a group or for a song. "Useless," just like that, with no qualifiers, so that everyone fits: men, women, and those who are neither men nor women, but who are).

OK. *Salud,* and (like it says on the cover of that fanzine that has the good taste to call itself "ZUPterraneo") what with so many things, "Something doesn't smell right," which means something like "there are things, and then there are things." *Salud!*

From the mountains of the Mexican Southeast,
The Sup, tuning up his guitar for the "special appearance."
Mexico, "other" and "different," October of 1999

THE TREE THAT IS THE MEXICAN NATION
FEBRUARY 26, 2001

Indigenous Brothers and Sisters of Oaxaca:
Brothers and Sisters of Oaxacan Civil Society:
Brothers and Sisters of the Democratic Teaching Profession:
Student Brothers and Sisters:
Religious Brothers and Sisters:
Worker Brothers and Sisters:
Campesino Brothers and Sisters:
Employed Brothers and Sisters:
Brother and Sister Bank Debtors:
Neighborhood Brothers and Sisters:
Housewife Sisters:
Small and Middle-sized Business Owner Brothers and Sisters:
Professional Brothers and Sisters:
Artist and Intellectual Brothers and Sisters:
Mexican Brothers and Sisters who have joined in on this March for Indigenous Dignity:
Brothers and Sisters from other countries who are accompanying us:

Through my voice speaks the voice of the Zapatista Army of National Liberation.

We wish to express our appreciation to the people of Oaxaca for the way they have treated us as brothers in struggle, the way we have been treated by them ever since we entered the lands of this state.

From Tepanatepec to this capital city of Oaxaca, everywhere we have received welcome and support from the population, primarily from the indigenous people.

The affection you have shown us—and which we believe we do not deserve—has moved us deeply.

We, the Zapatistas, the most small, those who live in the last corner of our homeland, have been made large by the strength that Oaxaca has given us.

I hope that one day we shall be able to respond with even a small part of the devotion and care which we have received.

We have learned much from you.

We have marveled at your organizational capacity, your fighting spirit, your sincere pride in the roots which give you color and name in these lands.

The Oaxacan indigenous communities make every indigenous person, in any part of Mexico, feel proud of being indigenous.

Knowing you up close has done nothing but confirm our conviction that the national indigenous movement is enjoying, right now, one of its best moments.

We hope that what all of us indigenous peoples of Mexico are seeking will indeed now be possible, and that the Indian peoples of these lands will have an important place here.

Thank you, people of Oaxaca!

The Zapatistas salute you!

Brothers and Sisters:

For many days now all Mexican indigenous people and all honest men and women of Mexico have been listening to a multitude of stupid remarks about our indigenous selves and our march, which we have called the March of Indigenous Dignity.

We all know whose voice it is that speaks such idiocies.

We know because we have been hearing them for centuries.

It is the voice of the one who brought deception and lies to our lands.

It is the voice of the one who imposed death and misery as indigenous state policy.

It is the voice of the one who yesterday used the whip and the sword to conquer our land, and who today uses modernization in order to do away with us.

It is the voice of stupidity.

It is the voice of ignorance.

It is the voice of arrogance.

It is the voice of the one who thinks he is superior to and stronger than we are.

It is the voice of the one who cannot conceive of any way of living other than at the cost of our deaths.

It is the voice of the one who says that the indigenous peoples will make progress only when they cease being indigenous.

The one who uses that voice, which threatens and persecutes us, is so blindly stupid that he considers a region of the country to have improved when the number of indigenous people residing in it has decreased.

Look at any government analysis and you will see that is how they have classified the country.

In addition, they have the cynicism to declare: "This region has already improved because there is now a greater mestizo population than before, and there are fewer indigenous people than before, or fewer people, that is, who speak an indigenous language."

And then we ask:

In the mind of the powerful: As more indigenous people disappear, the country develops more?

The development and modernization plans which the government praises: are they nothing more than plans to exterminate the indigenous peoples?

Do they, the powerful, believe that they are deceiving us and that they are doing something new?

Because their ways of thinking and methods are not at all different from those with which they tried to exterminate us five centuries ago, and they called their war of destruction and looting "civilization."

"Civilization" is what they called the destruction of our society and of our culture, the massacres of the indigenous peoples, the seizure of our lands and wealth, the humiliation of and contempt for our culture, the mockery of our language, rejection of our clothing, disgust for our dark color which is nothing other than the color of the earth.

Now the same war against us has taken another name, and it is called "modernization" by the one who is today the new foreman in the service of money.

But the powerful forget that those who wanted to exterminate us no longer exist, and we are here.

Indian peoples throughout Mexico are living...no, surviving...in the most shocking conditions of poverty.

The powerful say, "If they are in poverty it is because the indigenous people are lazy, run away from work, and waste what little they have."

"Lazy," they say to those who raised buildings, cities, great works, entire societies that were the marvel of the whole world before they were destroyed.

They say we waste what little we have, but they have been the ones who have looted our riches, those who have made the water filthy with the fecal waste of money, those who have destroyed the forests in order to traffic in wood, those who used up the minerals of our mountains, those who imposed crops which wore down and damaged the land, those who promoted the planting, trafficking and use of drugs, those who fattened themselves with our blood.

They are, in short, the ones who have destroyed our house with their ambition and force.

And now they blame us for not having a good house.

And so we would like to ask those powerful ones:

How many rich and powerful indigenous people are there in this country?

How many indigenous people are owners of industries that contaminate the water and damage the environment?

How many indigenous people have enriched themselves with the clandestine or brazen cutting down of trees?

How many indigenous people own mines?

How many indigenous people have agro-industries?

How many indigenous people are leaders of drug cartels?

How many indigenous people have made themselves powerful by exploiting other indigenous people?

How many indigenous people have devoted themselves to persecuting, torturing, imprisoning, corrupting, deceiving and assassinating other indigenous people?

No, it has not been we who have destroyed our house.

It has been they, the man-eaters, those with two faces, those of the sticky fingers, the fathers of the lies.

Before they arrived, dealing out death and destruction, the wealth of the earth was not lusted after.

Because the wealth of the earth was the wealth of the one who inhabited it, and the one who stole it was only stealing from himself.

And that stupidity of stealing the wealth of the earth is what they are offering us as "modernity?"

And then they call us, the indigenous people, "ignorant."

Did we not care for the land before they arrived?

Did we not care for our mother?

Did they not turn her into a prostitute, young and carefree before, and today dried up and old?

Did we invent the methods of over-exploitation of natural resources?

Are we the ignorant ones?

Does doing everything to totally destroy the only house one has mean being wise?

Because up until now no one has discovered another habitable planet, and so this is the only one we have.

Perhaps words have changed quite a bit.

Because, for us, the one who seeks his brothers' and his own ruin is stupid and ignorant.

Because, for us, the one who seeks his own progress, and that of others, is wise and intelligent.

But they, nonetheless, keep us away from technical and scientific knowledge.

Why?

Only because our color is the color of the earth?

Or because our indigenous way of thinking leads us to believe that the best possible way to take care of the earth, and to improve oneself, is by using science and technology?

Because our sense of community collides with their individualist sentiment?

Because it is easier to deceive, loot, and defeat one person who is alone, than the many who are united collectively?

The powerful call us "ignorant," and say that our beliefs concerning work and collective benefit are the products of foreign, communist, and subversive ideas.

Perhaps they are unaware that collective work and benefit already existed in these lands long before the foreigner "discovered" us.

The powerful call us "lazy," and say that our hands are only good for making crafts.

Perhaps they are unaware that, since before their long war against us, we have been making things they could not even imagine.

So great are, and were, our works.

The powerful does not think, but he has money to buy someone to think for him.

And then those purchased thoughts say: "The indigenous people want to return to the past. They want to exchange the tractor for the hoe, scientific knowledge for magic, paid work for slavery, to promote the buying and selling of women, to exchange free elections for chieftanship."

No, we do not want to return to the past.

Those purchased thoughts should not tire themselves out thinking.

We live in the past.

We have hoes and not tractors.

We do not have schools nor universities in order to shut them down, strangling their budget or with the Federal Preventive Police.

Our women are fighting for their gender rights.

We have slavery and the powerful are the masters.

We do not want to return to the past.

Nor do we want to continue living and dying in it.

We want science and technology, not in order to kill the earth and good thinking, but to make it better and richer.

We want to free ourselves from the slavery which the powerful subject us to, but not to make ourselves like the powerful—stupid and evil.

We want to live in the present and to build a future with everyone.

What we do not want is to cease being indigenous.

We are proud of being so.

We are proud of our language.

We are proud of our culture.

We are proud of our clothing.

We are proud of our struggle as women, as indigenous people, and as poor.

Proud of our methods of governing and governing ourselves.

Proud of our methods of working.

Proud, in short, of being the color of the earth.

That is why we want indigenous autonomy.

Not in order to separate ourselves from the country and to add one more poor country to those which already exist in abundance.

Not in order to return to a past from which we have not even been able to leave.

We want it in order to care for the earth with wisdom.

In order to make it rich and prosperous for us and for the entire country.

In order to avoid their looting it and destroying it and killing it.

In order to be able to work individually or collectively, but always taking care that one person does not profit to the detriment of others.

We want indigenous autonomy.

Not in order to create fundamentalist despots.

Not in order to replace the color of the earth with the color that is now humiliating us.

We want it so that the majority is valued all the time, and not occasionally.

So that the one who governs, governs by obeying.

So that governing is a responsibility and work for the collective, and not a means of enriching oneself at the cost of the governed.

So that indigenous women do not have to be marginalized for being indigenous or for being women.

So that the measure of political and economic success is no longer subjugating the "different ones" and forcing them to cease being what they are.

Not so that everyone will be like us.

But rather to be ourselves, respecting and being corrected by the others that are different from us.

Those of us who are the color of this Mexican earth want indigenous autonomy and we are going to achieve it.

No one will have any plans or programs which do not take us into account any longer.

No Puebla-Panama Plan, nor Trans-Isthmus megaproject, nor anything which means the selling or destruction of the house of the indigenous people which—it must not be forgotten—is part of the house of all Mexicans.

No longer will the color of one's skin, or the way of dress, or the language with which one clothes words, or the way one governs, or the relationship with land, be a reason for persecution, contempt, or marginalization.

We want indigenous autonomy because it is the only visible means of preventing this country from ending up in pieces and squandered.

Because it is the only visible means of saving Mexico from those who are proposing to finish it off as a nation, as a nation and who are trying to turn it into a high plateau of nostalgia of what was, and what could have been.

For Mexico, that is why we want indigenous autonomy.

Brothers and Sisters:

The eldest in these Oaxaca lands recount that the first man was born from the union of a tree. That the first man grew then, and he took good care of the tree that was his mother and father. That one day he realized the tree was head down, and he worked to put it where its roots should be, and thus the tree grew and never had to dry up and never had to die.

We are all part of the tree that is the Mexican nation.

But some of us are leaves, others flowers, others trunk, others branches, others fruit and others root which nurtures and gives foundation.

We are different, then, but we have one single life.

Tomorrow is only possible if it is inclusive.

But this country has had its head down. It has been determined, for almost two hundred years, to destroy its roots. How will it have a foundation if it destroys its roots?

The entire country must be turned right side up and put as it should be, so that it can, in that way, grow and never dry up and never die.

And so, if anyone asks what this March of Indigenous Dignity, the march of the color of the earth, wants, here is the answer:

Nothing more or less than that the entire country be turned right side up, and that it finally be made the tree where all of us who are different will have a common tomorrow as a nation, which is, also, the only possible tomorrow.

A tomorrow where all Mexicans, including the indigenous people, will have...

Democracy! Liberty! Justice!

Salud, Mixtec Brothers and Sisters! *Salud,* Cuicatec Brothers and Sisters! *Salud,* Zapotec Brothers and Sisters! *Salud,* Triqui Brothers and Sisters! *Salud,* Chocholtec Brothers and Sisters! *Salud,* Mazatec Brothers and Sisters! *Salud,* Mixe Brothers and Sisters! *Salud,* Chinantec Brothers and Sisters! *Salud,* Huave Brothers and Sisters! *Salud,* Zoque Brothers and Sisters! *Salud,* Chontal Brothers and Sisters! *Salud,* Tacuate Brothers and Sisters!

Salud, Nahua Brothers and Sisters! *Salud*, Ixcatec Brothers and Sisters! *Salud*, Amuzgo Brothers and Sisters! *Salud*, Chatino Brothers and Sisters! *Salud*, Black Brothers and Sisters! *Salud*, Oaxacan Brothers and Sisters!

From the dignified indigenous lands of Oaxaca,
Clandestine Revolutionary Indigenous Committee
General Command of the Zapatista Army of National Liberation.

MEXICO CITY: WE HAVE ARRIVED, WE ARE HERE
MARCH, 2001

Mexico City:

We have arrived.

We are here.

We are the National Indigenous Congress and Zapatistas who are, together, greeting you.

This grandstand, upon which we are standing, has not been placed where it is by accident. It is placed like this because, from the very beginning, the government has been at our backs.

Sometimes with artillery helicopters, sometimes with paramilitaries, sometimes with bomber planes, sometimes with war tanks, sometimes with soldiers, sometimes with the police, sometimes with offers for the buying and selling of consciences, sometimes with offers for surrender, sometimes with lies, sometimes with strident statements, sometimes with forgetting, sometimes with expectant silences. Sometimes, like today, with impotent silences.

That is why the government never sees us, that is why it does not listen to us.

If they quickened their pace a bit, they might catch up with us.

They could see us then, and listen to us.

They could understand the long and firm perspective of the one who is persecuted and who, nonetheless, is not worried, because he knows that it is the steps that follow which require attention and determination.

Brother, Sister:

Indigenous, worker, campesino, teacher, student, neighbor, house-wife, driver, fisherman, taxi driver, stevedore, office worker, street vendor, brother, unemployed, media worker, professional worker, religious person, homosexual, lesbian, transsexual, artist, intellectual, militant, activist, sailor, soldier, sportsman, legislator, bureaucrat, man, woman, child, young person, old one.

Brother, sister of the National Indigenous Congress, now rainbow of the best of the Indian peoples of Mexico:

We should not have been here.

(After hearing this, I'm sure that the one at my back is applauding like crazy for the first time. So I'm going to repeat it...)

We should not have been here.

The ones who should have been here are the Zapatista indigenous communities, their seven years of struggle and resistance, their ears and their eyes.

The Zapatista people. The men, children, women and old ones, support bases of the Zapatista Army of National Liberation, who are the feet that walk us, the voice that speaks us, the looking which makes us visible, the ear which makes us heard.

The ones who should have been here are the insurgent women and men, their persistent shadow, their silent strength, their memory risen.

The insurgent women and men. The women and men who make up the regular troops of the EZLN and who are guardian and heart of our peoples.

It is they who deserve to see you and to listen to you and to speak with you.

We should not have been here.

And, nonetheless, we are.

And we are next to them, the men and women who people the indigenous peoples of all Mexico.

The Indian peoples, our most first, the very first inhabitants, the first talkers, the first listeners.

Those who, being first, are the last to appear and to perish...

Indigenous brother, sister.

Tenek. We come from very far away.

Tlahuica. We walk time.

Tlapaneco. We walk the land.

Tojolabal. We are the bow and the arrow.

Totonaco. Wind walked.

Triqui. We are the blood and the heart.

Tzeltal. The warrior and the guardian.

Tzotzil. The embrace of the compañero.

Wixaritari. They assume us to be defeated.

Yaqui. Mute.

Zapoteco. Silenced.

Zoque. We have much time on our hands.

Maya. We came here to give ourselves a name.

Kumiai. We came here to say "we are."

Mayo. We came here to be gazed upon.

Mazahua. We are here to see ourselves being looked upon.

Mazateco. Our name is spoken here for our journey.

Mixe. This is what we are: The one who flourishes amidst hills. The one who sings. The one who guards and nurtures the ancient word. The one who speaks. The one who is of maize. The one who resides in the mountain. The one who walks the land. The one who shares the idea. The true we. The true man. The ancestor. The Lord of the net. The one who respects history. The one who is people of humble custom. The one who speaks flowers. The one who is rain. The one who has knowledge to govern. The hunter of arrows. The one who is sand. The one who is river. The one who is desert. The one who is the sea. The different one. The one who is person. The swift walker.

The one who is good. The one who is mountain. The one who is painted in color. The one who speaks the right word. The one who has three hearts. The one who is father and older brother. The one who walks the night. The one who works. The man who is man. The one who walks from the clouds. The one who has word. The one who shares the blood and the idea. The son of the sun. The one who goes from one side to the other. The one who walks the fog. The one who is mysterious. The one who works the word. The one who governs in the mountain. The one who is brother, sister.

Amuzgo. Our name says all of this.

Cora. And it says more.

Cuicateco. But it is hardly heard.

Chinanteco. Another name covers our name.

Chocholteco. We came here to be ourselves with those we are.

Chol. We are the mirror for seeing ourselves and for being ourselves.

Chontal. We, those who are the color of the earth.

Guarijío. Here, no longer shame for the color of our skin.

Huasteco. The language.

Huave. The clothing.

Kikapú. The dance.

Kukapá. The song.

Mame. The size.

Matlatzinca. The history.

Mixteco. Here, no longer embarrassment.

Nahuatl. Here, the pride of our being the color we are of the color of the earth.

Ñahñú. Here, the dignity which is seeing ourselves being seen being the color of the earth which we are.

O'Odham. Here, the voice which births us and inspires us.

Pame. Here, the silence no longer.

Popoluca. Here, the shout.

Purépecha. Here, the place that was concealed.

Rarámuri. Here, the dark light, the time and the feeling.

Indigenous Brother, Sister:
Non-indigenous Brother, Sister:

We are here to say we are here.

And when we say "we are here," we also name the other.

Brothers and sisters who are Mexican and who are not Mexican: With you we say "we are here," and we are with you.

We are a mirror.

We are here in order to see each other and to show each other, so you may look upon us, so you may look at yourself, so that the other looks in our looking. We are here and we are a mirror.

Not reality, but merely its reflection.

Not light, but merely a glimmer.
Not path, but merely a few steps.
Not guide, but merely one of the many routes which lead to tomorrow.

Brother, Sister, Mexico City:

When we say "we are," we are also saying "we are not," and "we shall not be."

That is why it is good for those who, up above, are money and the ones who peddle it, to take note of the word, to listen to it carefully, and to look with care at what they do not want to see.

We are not those who aspire to make themselves powerful and then impose the way and the word. We will not be.

We are not those who put a price on their own, or another's, dignity, and turn the struggle into a market, where politics is the business of sellers who are fighting, not about programs, but for clients. We will not be.

We are not those who are expecting pardon and handouts from the one who feigns to help, when he is, in reality, buying, and who does not pardon, but humiliates the one who, by merely existing, is a defiance, challenge, claim, and demand. We will not be.

We are not those who wait, naively, for justice to come from above, when it only comes from below. The liberty which can only be achieved with everyone. The democracy which is all the floors and is fought for all the time. We will not be.

We are not the passing fashion which, made ballad, is filed in the calendar of defeats which this country flaunts with such nostalgia. We will not be.

We are not the cunning calculation that falsifies the word and conceals a new fakery within it. We are not a simulated peace longing for eternal war.

We are, and we shall be, one more in the March.

Of Indigenous Dignity.

Of the Color of the Earth.

That which unveils and reveals the many Mexicos which are hidden, and suffer under Mexico.

We are not their spokesperson.

We are one voice among all those voices.

An echo which dignity repeats among all the voices.

We join with them, we are made multiple with them.

We will continue to be echo. We are, and we shall be, voice.

We are reflection and shout.

We shall always be.

We can be with or without a face, armed with fire or without, but we are Zapatistas, we are and we shall always be.

Ninety years ago the powerful asked those from below which Zapata was called:

"With whose permission, Señores?"

And those from below responded, and we respond:

"With ours."

And with our permission, for exactly 90 years, we have been shouting, and they call us "rebels."

And today we are repeating: we are rebels.

Rebels we shall be.
But we want to be so with everyone we are.

Without war as house and path.

So speaks the color of the earth: the struggle has many paths, and it has but one destiny: to be a color with all the colors which clothe the earth.

Brother, Sister:

Up there they say that this is the end of a tremor. That everything will pass except their being above us.

Up there they say that you are here to watch in morbid fascination, to hear, without listening to anything. They say we are few; that we are weak. That we are nothing more than a photograph, an anecdote, a spectacle, a perishable product whose expiration date is close at hand.

Up there they say that you will leave us alone. That we shall return alone and empty to the land in which we are.

Up there they say that forgetting is defeat, and they want to wait for you to forget, and to fail, and to be defeated.

They know up there, but they do not want to say it: there will be no more forgetting, and defeat shall not be the crown for the color of the earth.

But they do not want to say so, because saying it is recognizing it, and recognizing it is seeing that everything has changed, and nothing will change now without everyone changed, changing.

This movement, the one of the color of the earth, is yours, and because it is yours, it is ours.

This is what they fear: that there is no longer the "you," and the "we," because now we are all the color of the earth.

The hour has come for the Fox, and the one he serves, to listen to us.

The hour has come for the Fox, and the one who commands him, to see us. Our word says one single thing.

Our looking sees one single thing.

The constitutional recognition of indigenous rights and culture.

A dignified place for the color of the earth.

It is the hour in which this country ceases to be a disgrace, clothed only in the color of money.

It is the hour of the Indian peoples, of the color of the earth, of all the colors which we are and which we are in spite of the color of money.

We are rebels because the land rebels when someone buys and sells it, as if the physical land did not exist; as if the color of the earth did not exist.

Mexico City:

We are here. We are here as the rebellious color of the earth shouting:

Democracy!
Liberty!
Justice!

Mexico:

We did not come to tell you what to do, or to guide you along any path. We came in order to humbly, respectfully, ask you to help us. For you to not allow another day to dawn without this flag having an honorable place for us who are the color of the earth.

From the Zócalo in Mexico City.
Clandestine Revolutionary Indigenous Committee—
General Command of the Zapatista Army of National Liberation.

TO OPEN THE WORD
APRIL 2, 2001

Support bases of the Zapatista Army of National Liberation:
Local and regional Committees of the Zot'z Choj region of Chiapas:
Clandestine Revolutionary Indigenous Committee:
Compañero, compañera:

We have arrived now.

We are here in order to return the Comandantes and Comandantas of this region.

We have also come here in order to honor our dead.

We are here in order to salute the memory of three compañeros who died in 1994:

Compañero Sebastián Sántiz Gómez.
Compañero Severiano Sántiz Gómez.
Compañero Hermelindo Sántiz Gómez.
We are here in order to report to these dead compañeros.

And also to inform you, compañero, compañera.

You gave us the task of carrying your example of these fallen compañeros.

The example of not surrendering.

The example of not betraying.

The example of not selling oneself.

With the three examples we've carried, we've had to complete three missions.

The mission of pushing the three signals.

The mission of engaging in dialogue with civil society.

The mission of engaging with the Congress of the Union.

And thus I tell you that we did indeed carry out the three missions.

The three remaining military positions will now soon be free.

There are now just a few Zapatista prisoners remaining to be released.

The Cocopa law is now being discussed.

We have now spoken with the Congress of the Union.

We also spoke with hundreds of thousands of Mexican men and women.

In Chiapas. In Oaxaca. In Puebla. In Veracruz. In Tlaxcala. In Hidalgo. In Querétaro. In Guanajuato. In Michoacán. In the State of Mexico. In Morelos. In Guerrero. In the Federal District. In Mexico City.

We spoke with workers, campesinos, teachers, students, neighbors, housewives, drivers, fishermen, taxi drivers, office workers, employees, street vendors, brothers, the disabled, market vendors, unemployed, media workers, professional persons, religious persons, homosexuals and lesbians, artists, intellectuals, men, women, boys and girls, young people, old ones.

And we also spoke with many indigenous people.

As you commanded us, we were a mirror for the indigenous people of the entire country.

And they were a mirror for us.

They looked at themselves in our rebel dignity.

We looked at ourselves in their rebel dignity.

So it went with us and with them.

We understood that, in order to be looked upon, we have to look.

And, in order to look, one must open one's eyes.

And, in order to open one's eyes, the word must be opened.

For us, the Zapatistas, it was not easy to open the word.

We had to make a war.

Compañeros like Sebastián, Severiano, and Hermelindo had to die.

With those, and other deaths, we opened our word.

And, with our word, our eyes were also opened.

And in that way we could look at others.

And in that way we could demand that they look at us, that they listen to us.

It cost us war and blood for them to look at us, for them to listen to us.

While looking, and with the word given to us by our dead, we made this trip.

When we looked, our dead looked.

When we spoke, our dead spoke.

Looking and speaking now, we are also listening and we were looked at.

In our looking we saw many young people and children.

Because most of those who accompanied and supported this march were young people and children.

They came from all roads.

They gathered together in all the cities.

They came wanting to listen.

They came seeking.

They looked.

Because the one who listens is seeking.

Because the looking is what he is seeking.

He wants to find something.

He wants to find himself.

We spoke to the children and to the young people with the word of truth.

We told them clearly that we were not what they were seeking.

We were not, because we ourselves are also seeking.

We were seeking them and ourselves.

While seeking the one and the other, we found ourselves.

They found us.

We found them.

And, in finding us, we looked at ourselves.

And in them we saw the word which our dead had been speaking to us.

Because they had told us that the young people and the children were what we were seeking.

Hope.
Rebellion.
Generosity.

Commitment.

The morning.

And you must know, compañero, compañera,

That the children and young people were generous with us.

They committed themselves to us.

They rebelled with us.

And with us they shared the hope for the morning.

That is why I am telling you, compañero, compañera,

That we have much to be grateful for to our dead.

And we have much to be grateful for to the young people and to the children.

Because the ones and the others taught us to seek.

The ones and the others helped us to find, and to find ourselves.

And thus we are able to tell our dead here that they were indeed right.

That one day it shall indeed dawn.

That on that day there shall be no concealed faces.

That on that day the smile shall not be lost behind a mask.

And on that day our dead shall live.

And that day is going to dawn, thanks to the children and to the young people.

And that is why I am asking you, compañero, compañera,

For us to salute the children and young people.

The indigenous children and young people.

The non-indigenous young people and children.

Because in saluting them we are also saluting our dead.

And we salute them exactly as we salute our dead.

With a flower.

With a flower we tell them that they live.

With a flower we are telling ourselves that we live.

That our dead shall always live.

That death always dies.

Sebastián, Severiano, Hermelindo, children, young people:

Here is our salute.

Democracy! Liberty! Justice!

From the mountains of the Mexican Southeast,
Subcomandante Insurgente Marcos.

WOMEN WITHOUT FEAR

MAY 22, 2006

Words from the Sixth Committee of the EZLN for the public event "Women Without Fear. We Are All Atenco."

Good evening.

My name is Marcos, Subcomandante Insurgente Marcos.

For those of you who are familiar with Zapatismo, it might not be necessary to explain what I'm doing here, at an event of, and for, women.

Of course you are not just women, but women who have decided to raise your voices in order to protest against the attacks the police have been making, and are making, on other women since May 3rd and 4th, 2006 in San Salvador Atenco, in the State of Mexico, in the Mexican Republic.

You are, here, there, and everywhere, women without fear.

My name is Subcomandante Insurgente Marcos, and I am, among other things, the spokesperson for the EZLN, a primarily indigenous organization which fights for democracy, liberty and justice for our country, which is called Mexico.

As spokesperson for the EZLN, those others take voice through my voice, those who comprise us, who give us face, word, heart.

A collective voice.

In that collective voice is the voice of Zapatista women.

I am called Marcos, and among the numerous personal flaws I bear, sometimes cynically and cockily, is that of being man, macho, male.

As such I must bear, and often flaunt, a series of archetypes, clichés, proofs.

Not only in regard to me and my sex, but also and above all in reference to woman, the female gender.

To those flaws which define me personally, someone might add the one we have as Zapatistas, to wit: that of still not having lost the capacity for being astonished, for being amazed.

As Zapatistas, sometimes we approach other voices, which we know to be different, strange, and yet similar and appropriate.

Voices which astonish and amaze our ear with your light...and with your shadow.

Voices, for example, of women.

From the collective which gives us face and name, journey and path, we go to great effort in choosing where to direct our ears and hearts.

And so now we are choosing to hear the voice of women who have no fear.

Can one listen to a light? And, if so, can one listen to a shadow?

And who else chooses, as we are today, to lend ear—and with it, thought and heart—in order to listen to those voices?

We choose. We choose to be here, to listen to and make echo for an injustice committed against women.

We choose to be fearless in order to listen to those who are not afraid to speak.

The brutality wielded by the bad Mexican governments in San Salvador Atenco on the 3rd and 4th of May, and which is still going on, to this very night, against the prisoners, especially the violence against women, is what summons us.

And not only that. Those bad governments are trying to sow fear through their actions, and, no, what is happening now is that they are sowing indignation and anger.

In a newspaper this morning, one of the individuals who, along with Vicente Fox and his cabinet, are priding themselves on "imposing the Rule of Law," Señor Peña Nieto (alleged Governor of the State of Mexico) stated that what happened at Atenco had been planned.

If this were so, then those who were beaten, illegally detained, sexually attacked, raped, humiliated, then they planned these victims, among other things, to be women.

We know, from the statements of those without fear who were detained, who are our compañeras, that they were attacked as women, their bodies violated.

And we also know from their words that the violence visited upon their bodies brought pleasure to the policemen.

The woman's body taken violently, usurped, attacked in order to obtain pleasure.

And the promise of that pleasure taken on those women's bodies was the extra benefit which the police received along with the mandate to "impose peace and order" in Atenco.

Certainly according to the government they planned on having the body of a woman, and, they planned, with extreme depravity, that their bodies would be plundered for the "forces of law."

Señor Fox, the federal leader of "change" and of the "Rule of Law," clarified for us a few months ago that women are "two-legged washing machines."

And it so happens that up above those machines of pleasure and of work, which are the bodies of women, include assembly instructions which the dominant system assigns them.

If a human being is born woman, she must travel throughout her life a path which has been built especially for her.

Being a girl. Being an adolescent. Being a young woman. Being an adult. Being mature. Being old.

And not just from menarche to menopause. Capitalism has discovered they can obtain objects of work and pleasure in infancy and in old age, and we have "Gobers Preciosos" (pedophile governors) and pedophile businessmen everywhere for the appropriation and administration of those objects.

Women, they say above, should travel through life begging pardon and asking permission for being, and in order to be, women.

And traveling a path full of barbed wire.

A path which must be traveled by crawling, with head and heart against the ground.

And, even so, despite following the assembly instructions, gathering scrapes, wounds, scars, blows, amputations, death.

And seeking the one responsible for those sorrows in oneself, because condemnation is also included in the crimes of being women.

In the assembly instructions for the merchandise known as "Woman," it explains that the model should always have her head bowed. That her most productive position is on her knees. That the brain is optional, and its inclusion is often counterproductive. That her heart should be nourished with trivialities. That her spirit should be maintained by competition with others of her same gender in order to attract the buyer, that always unsatisfied customer who is the male. That her ignorance should be fed in order to guarantee better functioning. That the product is capable of self-maintenance and improvement (and there is a wide range of products for that, in addition to salons and metal and painting workshops). That she should not only learn to reduce her vocabulary to "yes" and "no," but, above all, she should learn when she should speak these words.

There is a warranty included in the assembly instructions for the product called "Woman" that she will always have her head lowered.

And that, if for some involuntary or premeditated manufacturing defect, one should lift her gaze, then the implacable scythe of power will chop off the place of thought, and condemn her to walking as if being a woman were something for which one must ask forgiveness and for which one must ask permission.

In order to comply with this warranty, there are governments who substitute the weapons and sex of their police officers for their lack of brains. And, in addition, these same governments have mental hospitals, jails and cemeteries for irreparably "broken" women.

A bullet, a punch, a penis, prison bars, a judge, a government, in sum, a system, puts a sign on a woman who doesn't ask for forgiveness or permission which reads: "Out of Service. Non-Recyclable Product."

Women must ask permission in order to be a woman, and it is granted to her if she is so according to what is shown in the assembly instructions.

Women should serve men, always following those instructions, in order to be absolved of the crime of being a woman.

At home, in the fields, the street, the school, work, transportation, culture, art, entertainment, science, government. Twenty-four hours a day and 365 days a year. From when they are born until they die, women confront this assembly process.

But there are women who confront it with rebellion.

Women who, instead of asking permission, command their own existence.

Women who, instead of begging pardon, demand justice.

Because the assembly instructions say that women should be submissive and walk on their knees.

And, nonetheless, some women are naughty and walk upright.

There are women who tear up the assembly instructions and stand up on their feet.

There are women without fear.

They say that when a woman moves forward, no man moves back.

It depends, I say, from my machismo reloaded perspective—a mixture of Pedro Infante and Jose Alfredo Jimenez.

It depends, for example, on whether the man is in front of the woman who is moving forward.

My name is Marcos, I have the personal flaw of being man, macho, male. And the collective virtue of being what we are, we who are Zapatistas.

As such, I confess that I am astonished and amazed at seeing a woman raise herself up and seeing the assembly instructions shattering, torn into pieces.

A woman standing up is so beautiful that it makes one shiver just to look at her.

And that is what listening is, learning to look...

Salud to these women, to our imprisoned compañeras and to those who are gathered here.

Salud for your having no fear.

Salud for the valor which you pass on to us, for the conviction you grant us that if we do nothing to change this system, we are all accomplices in it.

From the Other City of Mexico,
Subcomandante Insurgente Marcos.

P.S. WHICH ASKS: What punishment do those officials, leaders, and police deserve who attacked the women, our compañeras, like that? What punishment does the system deserve which has turned being a woman into a crime? If we are silent, if we look the other way, if we allow the police brutality in Atenco to go unpunished, who will be safe? Isn't the release of all the Atenco prisoners thus a matter of elemental justice?

HOW BIG IS THE WORLD?
FEBRUARY, 2006

After a day of preparation meetings for the Other Campaign (it was September, it was dawn, there was rain from a far-off cloud), we were heading towards the hut where our things were when we ran into a citizen who all of a sudden came out with: "Listen, Sup, what are the Zapatistas proposing?" Without even stopping, I answered: "Changing the world." We reached the hut and began getting things ready in order to leave. Insurgenta Erika waited until I was alone. She approached me and said "Listen, Sup, the world is very big," as if she were trying to make me realize what nonsense I was proposing and that I didn't, in reality, know what I was saying when I'd said what I'd said. Following the custom of responding to a question with another question, I came out with:

"How big?"

She kept looking at me, and she answered almost tenderly: "Very big."

I insisted: "Yes, but how big?"

She thought about it for a minute and said: "Much bigger than Chiapas."

Then they told us we had to go. When we had gotten back, in the barracks now and after making Penguin comfortable, Erika came over to me, carrying a globe, the kind they use in elementary schools. She put it on the ground and told me: "Look, Sup, here, in this little piece, there's Chiapas, and all this is the world," almost caressing the globe with her dark hands as she said it.

"Hmm," I said, lighting my pipe in order to gain some time.

Erika insisted: "Now you've seen that it's very big?"

"Yes, but we're not going to change it all by ourselves, we're going to change it with many compañeros and compañeras from everywhere." At that point they called the guard. Showing that I'd learned, she shot back at me before she left: "How many compañeros and compañeras?"

How big is the world?

In the Tehuacán valley, in the Sierra Negra, in the Sierra Norte, in the suburban areas of Puebla. From the most forgotten corners of the other Puebla, answers are ventured:

In Altepexi, a young woman replied: More than 12 hours a day of work in the *maquiladora*, working on days off, no benefits, or insurance, or Christmas bonus, or profit sharing. Authoritarianism and bad treatment by the manager or line supervisor, being punished by not being paid when I get sick, seeing my name on a blacklist so they won't give me work in any *maquiladora*. If we mobilize, the owner closes down and goes someplace else. Transportation is very bad, and I get back to the house where I live really late. I look at the light bill, the water bill, taxes, I add them up and see there's not enough. Realizing that there's not even any water to drink, that the plumbing doesn't work and the street stinks. And the next day, after sleeping badly and being poorly fed, back to work. The world is as big as the rage I feel against all this.

A young Mixtec indigenous girl: My papa went to the United States more than 12 years ago. My mama works sewing balls. They pay her 10 pesos for each ball, and if one of them isn't good, they charge 40 pesos. They don't pay them, not until the contractor comes back to the village. My brother is also packing to leave. We women are alone in this, in carrying on with the family, the land, the work. And so it's up to us to also carry on with the struggle. The world is as big as the courage this injustice makes me feel, so big it makes my blood boil.

In San Miguel Tzinacapan an elderly couple look at each other and answer almost in unison: the world is the size of our effort to change it.

An indigenous campesino from the Sierra Negra, a veteran of all the dislocations, except the dislocation of history: It has to be very big, that's why we need to make our organization grow.

In Ixtepec, Sierra Norte: The world is the size of the swinishness of the bad governments and of the Antorcha Campesina, which is just prejudiced against the campesino and is still poisoning the earth.

In Huitziltepec, from a small autonomous school, a rebel television station is broadcasting a truth: the world is so large that it has room for the history of the community and of its desire and struggle to continue looking out at the universe with dignity. A lady, an indigenous artisan, from the same ground as the departed Comandanta Ramona, adds off-mike: "The world is as big as the injustice we feel, because they pay us a pittance for what we do, and we watch the things we need just pass us by, because there's not enough."

In the neighborhood of Granja: It can't be very big, because it seems as if there's no room for poor children, they just scold us, persecute and beat us, and we're just trying to make enough to eat.

In Coronango: As big as the world is, it's dying from the neoliberal pollution of the land, water, air. It's breaking down, because that's what our grandparents said, that when the community breaks down, the world breaks down.

In San Matías Cocoyotla: It's as big as the government's lack of shame, which is simply destroying what we do as workers. Now we have to organize in order to defend ourselves from the government which is supposed to serve us. Now they see that they are without shame.

In Puebla, but in the other Puebla: The world isn't so big because what the rich already have isn't enough for them, and now they want to take away from us poor people what little we have.

Again, another Puebla, a young woman: It's very big, so just a few of us can't change it. We all have to join together in order to do it, because if not, we can't, you get tired.

A young artist: It's big, but it's rotten. They extort money from us for being young people. In this world it's a crime to be young.

A neighbor: However big it may be, it's small for the rich, because they are invading communal lands, *ejidos*, popular neighborhoods. As if there's no longer enough room for their shopping centers and their luxuries, and they're putting them on our lands. The same way, I believe, that there's no room for us, those from below.

A worker: The world is as big as the cynicism of the corrupt leaders. And they still say they're for the defense of the workers. And up above they've got their shit together: whether it's the owner, the official or the pro-management union leader, no matter what new things they say. They should make one of those landfills, a garbage dump, and put all of them in it together. Or not, better not, because they'd certainly pollute everything. And then if we were to put them in jail, the criminals would riot because even they don't want to live next to those bastards.

Now it's dawn in this other Puebla which hasn't ceased to amaze us with every step we take on its lands. We've just finished eating, and I'm thinking about what I'm going to say on this occasion. Suddenly a little suitcase is sticking out from under the door, and it almost immediately gets stuck in the crack. A murmur of heavy breathing can barely be heard, of someone pushing from the other side. The little suitcase finally makes it through and, behind it, stumbling, something appears which looks remarkably like a beetle. If it weren't for the fact that I was in Puebla, albeit the other Puebla, and not in the mountains of the Mexican southeast, I would almost swear that it was Durito. As if putting aside a bad thought, I return to the notebook where the question which headed this surprise exam is already written down. I continue trying to write, but nothing worthwhile occurs to me. That is what I was doing, making a fool of myself, when I felt as if something were on my shoulder. I was just about to shrug in order to get rid of it, when I heard:

"Do you have tobacco?"

"That little voice, that little voice," I thought.

"What little voice? I see you're jealous of my masculine and seductive voice," Durito protested.

There was no longer any room for doubt, and so, with more resignation than enthusiasm, I said:

"Durito...!"

"Not 'Durito'! I am the greatest righter of wrongs, the savior of the helpless, the comforter of the defenseless, the hope of the weak, the unattainable dream of women, the favorite poster of children, the object of men's unspeakable jealousy, the..."

"Stop it, stop it! You sound like a candidate in an election campaign," I told Durito, trying to interrupt him. Uselessly, as can be seen, because he continued:

"...the most gallant of that race which has embraced errant knighthood: Don Durito of the Lacandona, Inc. And authorized by the good government assemblies."

As he said this, Durito showed me a decal on his shell which read: "Authorized by the Charlie Parker Rebel Zapatista Autonomous Municipality (MAREZ)."

"Charlie Parker? I didn't know we had a MAREZ with that name, at least we didn't when I left," I said disconcertedly.

"Of course, I established it just before I left there and came to your aid," Durito said.

"How odd, I asked them to send me tobacco, not a beetle," I responded.

"I am not a beetle, I am a knight errant who has come to get you out of the predicament you find yourself in."

"Me? Predicament?"

"Yes, do not act like Mario Marán's 'precious hero' in the face of those recordings which revealed his true moral caliber. Are you in a predicament or not?"

"Well, predicament, what's called a predicament, then…yes, I'm in a predicament."

"You see? Perhaps you were not longing for me, the very best of the knights errant, to come to your aid?"

I thought for barely an instant and responded:

"Well, the truth is, no."

"Come, do not conceal that great pleasure, the huge joy and the unbridled enthusiasm which exists in your heart upon seeing me once again."

"I prefer to conceal it," I said resignedly.

"Fine, fine, enough of the welcoming fiestas and fireworks. Who is the scoundrel I should defeat with the arm I have below and to the left? Where are the Kamel Nacifs, Succar Kuris so-and-sos, and others of such low ilk?"

"No scoundrels and nothing to do with that ilk of swine. I have to answer a question."

"Come on," Durito pressed.

"How big is the world?" I asked.

"Well, there is a short version and a long version of the answer. Which do you want?"

I looked at my watch. It was 3 AM, and my eyelids and cap were falling into my eyes, and so I said without hesitation:

"The short version."

"What do you mean, the short version! Do you think I have been following your tracks through eight states of the Mexican Republic in order to present the short version? No way José, nor can Durito, not hardly, absolutely not, no way, negative, rejected, no."

"Fine," I said, resigned. "The long version then."

"That's it, my big-nosed nomad! Take this down."

I picked up my pen and notebook. Durito dictated:

"If you look at it from above, the world is small and the green color of the dollar. It fits perfectly in the price indexes and the valuations of a stock market, in the profits of a transnational corporation, in the election polls of a country which has suffered the hijacking of its dignity, in the cosmopolitan calculator which adds capital and subtracts lives, mountains, rivers, seas, springs, histories, entire civilizations, in the miniscule brain of George W. Bush, in the shortsightedness of savage capitalism badly dressed up in neoliberal attire. Seen from above, the world is very small because it disregards persons and, in their place, there is a bank account number, with no movement other than that of deposits.

But if you look at it from below, the world stretches so far that one look is not enough to encompass it, instead many looks are necessary in order to complete it. Seen from below, the world abounds in worlds, almost all of them painted with the color of dislocation, poverty, despair, death. The world below grows sideways, especially to the left side, and it has many colors, almost as many as persons and histories. And it grows backwards, to the history which the world below made. And it grows towards itself with the struggles that illuminate it, even though the light from above goes out. And it sounds, even though the silence of above crushes it. And it grows forward, divining in every heart the morrow that will be given birth by those who below are who they are. Seen from below, the world is so big that many worlds fit, and, even so, there is space left over, for example, for a jail.

Or, in summary, seen from above, the world shrinks, and nothing fits in it other than injustice. And, seen from below, the world is so spacious that there is room for joy, music, song, dance, dignified work, justice, everyone's opinions and thoughts, no matter how different they are, if below they are what they are."

I had barely been able to write it down. I re-read Durito's response, and I asked him:

"And what is the short version?"

"The short version is the following: the world is as big as the heart which first hurts and then struggles, along with everyone from below and to the left."

Durito left. I continued writing while the moon waned in the heavens with the night's damp caress...

I would like to venture a response. Imagining that I, with my hands, undo her hair and her desire, that I envelope her ear with a sigh, and, while my lips move up and down her hills, understanding that the world is as large as is my thirst for her belly.

Or, more decorously, trying to say that the world is as large as the delirium to make it "otherly," as the ear that is needed to embrace all the voices of below, as this other collective desire to go against the tide, uniting rebellions from below, while above they separate solitudes.

The world is as big as the prickly plant of indignation which we raise, knowing the flower of tomorrow will be born from it. And, in that tomorrow, the Iberoamerican University will be a public, free, and secular university, and in its corridors and rooms will be the workers, campesinos, indigenous students and others who today are outside.

That is all. Your responses should be presented on February 30th in triplicate: one for your conscience, another for the Other Campaign, and another with a heading that clearly states: Warning, for those of above who believe, naively, that they are eternal.

From the other Puebla,
Sup Marcos,
Sixth Committee of the EZLN.
Mexico.

BETWEEN LIGHT AND SHADOW
MAY 24, 2014

In La Realidad (Reality), Planet Earth

Compañera, compañeroa, compañero:

Good evening, afternoon, or morning, whichever it may be in
your geography, time, and way of being.

Good very early morning.

I would like to ask the compañeras, compañeros and compañeroas
of the Sixth who came from other places, especially the
compañeros from the independent media, for your patience,
tolerance, and understanding for what I am about to say, because
these will be the final words that I speak in public before I cease
to exist.

I am speaking to you and to those who listen to and look at us
through you.

Perhaps at the start, or as these words unfold, the sensation will
grow in your heart that something is out of place, that something
doesn't quite fit, as if you were missing one or various pieces that
would help make sense of the puzzle that is about to be revealed
to you. As if indeed what is missing is still pending.

Maybe later—days, weeks, months, years or decades later—what we are about to say will be understood.

My compañeras and compañeros at all levels of the EZLN do not worry me, because this is indeed our way here: to walk and to struggle, always knowing that what is missing is yet to come.

What's more, and without meaning to offend anyone, the intelligence of the Zapatista compas is way above average.

In addition, it pleases and fills us with pride that this collective decision will be made known in front of compañeras, compañeros and compañeroas, both of the EZLN and of the Sixth.

And how wonderful that it will be through the free, alternative, and independent media that this archipelago of pain, rage, and dignified struggle—what we call "the Sixth"—will hear what I am about to say, wherever they may be.

If anyone else is interested in knowing what happened today, they will have to go to the independent media to find out.

So, here we go. Welcome to the Zapatista reality (La Realidad).

I. A DIFFICULT DECISION.

When we erupted and interrupted in 1994 with blood and fire, it was not the beginning of war for us as Zapatistas.

The war from above, with its death and destruction, its dispossession and humiliation, its exploitation and the silence it imposed on the defeated, we had been enduring for centuries.

What began for us in 1994 is one of many moments of war by those below against those above, against their world.

This war of resistance is fought day-in and day-out in the streets of any corner of the five continents, in their countryside and in their mountains.

It was and is ours, as it is of many from below, a war for humanity and against neoliberalism.

Against death, we demand life.

Against silence, we demand the word and respect.

Against oblivion, memory.

Against humiliation and contempt, dignity.

Against oppression, rebellion.

Against slavery, freedom.

Against imposition, democracy.

Against crime, justice.

Who with the least bit of humanity in their veins would or could question these demands?

And many listened to us then.

The war we waged gave us the privilege of arriving to attentive and generous ears and hearts in geographies near and far.

Even lacking what was then lacking, and as of yet missing what is yet to come, we managed to attain the other's gaze, their ear, and their heart.

It was then that we saw the need to respond to a critical question.

"What next?"

In the gloomy calculations on the eve of war there hadn't been any possibility of posing any question whatsoever. And so this question brought us to others:

Should we prepare those who come after us for the path of death?

Should we develop more and better soldiers?

Invest our efforts in improving our battered war machine?

Simulate dialogues and a disposition toward peace while preparing new attacks?

Kill or die as the only destiny?

Or should we reconstruct the path of life, that which those from above had broken and continue breaking?

The path that belongs not only to indigenous people, but to workers, students, teachers, youth, peasants, along with all of those differences that are celebrated above and persecuted and punished below.

Should we have adorned with our blood the path that others have charted to power, or should we have turned our heart and gaze toward who we are, toward those who are what we are—that is, the indigenous people, guardians of the earth and of memory?

Nobody listened then, but in the first babblings that were our words we made note that our dilemma was not between negotiating and fighting, but between dying and living.

Whoever noticed then that this early dilemma was not an individual one would have perhaps better understood what has occurred in the Zapatista reality over the last 20 years.

But I was telling you that we came across this question and this dilemma.

And we chose.

And rather than dedicating ourselves to training guerrillas, soldiers, and squadrons, we developed education and health promoters, who went about building the foundations of autonomy that amaze the world today.

Instead of constructing barracks, improving our weapons, and building walls and trenches, we built schools, hospitals and health centers, improving our living conditions.

Instead of fighting for a place in the Parthenon of individualized deaths of those from below, we chose to construct life.

All this in the midst of a war that was no less lethal because it was silent.

Because, compas, it is one thing to yell, "You Are Not Alone," and another to face an armed column of federal troops with only one's body, which is what happened in the Highlands zone of Chiapas. And then if you are lucky someone finds out about it, and with a little more luck the person who finds out is outraged, and then with another bit of luck the outraged person does something about it.

In the meantime, the tanks are held back by Zapatista women, and in the absence of ammunition, insults and stones would force the serpent of steel to retreat.

And in the Northern zone of Chiapas, to endure the birth and development of the *guardias blancas* [armed thugs traditionally hired by landowners] who would then be recycled as paramilitaries; and in the Tzotz Choj Zone, the continual assault of peasant organizations who have no sign of being "independent" even in name; and in the Selva Tzeltal zone, the combination of the paramilitaries and contras [anti-Zapatistas].

It is one thing to say, "We Are All Marcos" or "We Are Not All Marcos," depending on the situation, and quite another to endure persecution with all of the machinery of war: the invasion of communities, the "combing" of the mountains, the use of trained attack dogs, the whirling blades of armed helicopters destroying the crests of the ceiba trees, the "Wanted: Dead or Alive" that was born in the first days of January 1994 and reached its most hysterical level in 1995 and in the remaining years of the administration of that now-employee of a multinational corporation, which this Border Jungle zone suffered as of 1995 and to which must be added the same sequence of aggressions from peasant organizations, the use of paramilitaries, militarization, and harassment.

If there exists a myth today in any of this, it is not the ski mask, but the lie that has been repeated from those days onward, and even taken up by highly educated people, that the war against the Zapatistas lasted only 12 days.

I will not provide a detailed retelling. Someone with a bit of critical spirit and seriousness can reconstruct the history, and add and subtract to reach the bottom line, and then say if there are and ever were more reporters than police and soldiers; if there was more flattery than threats and insults, if the price advertised was to see the ski mask or to capture him "dead or alive."

Under these conditions, at times with only our own strength and at other times with the generous and unconditional support of good people across the world, we moved forward in the construction—still incomplete, true, but nevertheless defined—of what we are.

So it isn't just an expression, a fortunate or unfortunate one depending on whether you see from above or from below, to say, "Here we are, the dead of always, dying again, but this time in order to live." It is reality.

And almost 20 years later...

On December 21, 2012, when the political and the esoteric coincided, as they have at other times in preaching catastrophes that are meant, as they always are, for those from below, we repeated the sleight of hand of January of '94 and, without firing a single shot, without arms, with only our silence, we once again humbled the arrogant pride of the cities that are the cradle and hotbed of racism and contempt.

If on January 1, 1994, it was thousands of faceless men and women who attacked and defeated the garrisons that protected the cities, on December 21, 2012, it was tens of thousands who took, without words, those buildings where they celebrated our disappearance.

The mere indisputable fact that the EZLN had not only not been weakened, much less disappeared, but rather had grown quantitatively and qualitatively would have been enough for any moderately intelligent mind to understand that, in these 20 years, something had changed within the EZLN and the communities.

Perhaps more than a few people think that we made the wrong choice; that an army cannot and should not endeavor toward peace.

We made that choice for many reasons, it's true, but the primary one was and is because this is the way that we [as an army] could ultimately disappear.

Maybe it's true. Maybe we were wrong in choosing to cultivate life instead of worshipping death.

But we made the choice without listening to those on the outside. Without listening to those who always demand and insist on a fight to the death, as long as others will be the ones to do the dying.

We made the choice while looking and listening inward, as the collective Votán that we are.

We chose rebellion, that is to say life.

That is not to say that we didn't know that the war from above would try and would keep trying to re-assert its domination over us.

We knew and we know that we would have to repeatedly defend what we are and how we are.

We knew and we know that there will continue to be death in order for there to be life.

We knew and we know that in order to live, we die.

II. A FAILURE?

They say out there that we haven't achieved anything for ourselves.

It never ceases to surprise us that they hold on to this position with such self-assurance.

They think that the sons and daughters of the comandantes and comandantas should be enjoying trips abroad, studying in private schools, and achieving high posts in business or political realms. That instead of working the land and producing their food with sweat and determination, they should shine in social networks, amuse themselves in clubs, show off in luxury.

Maybe the subcomandantes should procreate and pass their jobs, perks, and stages onto their children, as politicians from across the spectrum do.

Maybe we should, like the leaders of the CIOAC-H and other peasant organizations do, receive privileges and payment in the form of projects and monetary resources, keeping the largest part for ourselves while leaving the bases [of support] with only a few crumbs, in exchange for following the criminal orders that come from above.

Well it's true, we haven't achieved any of this for ourselves.

While difficult to believe, 20 years after that "Nothing For Ourselves," it didn't turn out to be a slogan, a good phrase for posters and songs, but rather a reality, the reality.

If being accountable is what marks failure, then unaccountability is the path to success, the road to power.

But that's not where we want to go.

It doesn't interest us.

Within these parameters, we prefer to fail than to succeed.

III. THE HANDOFF, OR CHANGE.

In these 20 years, there has been a multiple and complex handoff, or change, within the EZLN.

Some have only noticed the obvious: the generational change.

Today, those who were small or had not even been born at the beginning of the uprising are the ones carrying the struggle forward and directing the resistance.

But some of the experts have not considered other changes:

That of class: from the enlightened middle class to the indigenous peasant.

That of race: from mestizo leadership to a purely indigenous leadership.

And the most important: the change in thinking: from revolutionary vanguardism to "governing by obeying;" from taking power Above to the creation of power below; from professional politics to everyday politics; from the leaders to the people; from the marginalization of gender to the direct participation of women; from the mocking of the other to the celebration of difference.

I won't expand more on this because the course "Freedom According to the Zapatistas" was precisely the opportunity to confirm whether in organized territory, the celebrity figure is valued over the community.

Personally, I don't understand why thinking people who affirm that history is made by the people get so frightened in the face of an existing government of the people where "specialists" are nowhere to be seen.

Why does it terrify them so that the people command, that they are the ones who determine their own steps?

Why do they shake their heads with disapproval in the face of "rule by obeying?"

The cult of individualism finds in the cult of vanguardism its most fanatical extreme.

And it is this precisely—that the indigenous people rule, and now with an indigenous person as the spokesperson and chief — that terrifies them, repels them, and finally sends them looking for someone requiring vanguards, bosses, and leaders. Because there is also racism on the left, above all within that left which claims to be revolutionary.

The ezetaelene is not of this kind. That's why not just anybody can be a Zapatista.

IV. A CHANGING AND MALLEABLE HOLOGRAM. THAT WHICH WILL NOT BE.

Before the dawn of 1994, I spent 10 years in these mountains. I met and personally interacted with some whose death we all died. Since then, I know and interact with others that are today here with us.

In many of the smallest hours of the morning I found myself trying to digest the stories that they told me, the worlds that they sketched with their silences, hands, and gazes, their insistence in pointing to something else, something further.

Was it a dream, that world so other, so distant, so foreign?

Sometimes I thought that they had gone ahead of us all, that the words that guided and guide us came from times that didn't have a calendar, that were lost in imprecise geographies: always with the dignified south omnipresent in all the cardinal points.

Later I learned that they weren't telling me about an inexact, and therefore, improbable world.

That world was already unfolding.

And you? Did you not see it? Do you not see it?

We have not deceived anyone from below. We have not hidden

the fact that we are an army, with its pyramidal structure, its central command, its decisions hailing from above to below. We didn't deny what we are in order to ingratiate ourselves with the libertarians or to move with the trends.

But anyone can see now whether ours is an army that supplants or imposes.

And I should say that I have already asked compañero Subcomandante Insurgente Moisés' permission to say this:

Nothing that we've done, for better or for worse, would have been possible without an armed military, the Zapatista Army for National Liberation; without it we would not have risen up against the bad government, exercising the right to legitimate violence: The violence of below in the face of the violence of above.

We are warriors and as such we know our role and our moment.

In the earliest hours of the morning on the first day of the first month of the year 1994, an army of giants, that is to say, of indigenous rebels, descended on the cities to shake the world with its step.

Only a few days later, with the blood of our fallen soldiers still fresh on the city streets, we noticed that those from outside did not see us.

Accustomed to looking down on the indigenous people from above, they didn't lift their gaze to look at us.

Accustomed to seeing us humiliated, their heart did not understand our dignified rebellion.

Their gaze had stopped on the only mestizo they saw with a ski mask, that is, they didn't see.

Our authorities, our commanders, then said to us:

"They can only see those who are as small as they are. Let's make someone as small as they are, so that they can see him and through him, they can see us."

And so began a complex maneuver of distraction, a terrible and marvelous magic trick, a malicious move from the indigenous heart that we are, with indigenous wisdom challenging one of the bastions of modernity: the media.

And so began the construction of the character named "Marcos."

I ask that you follow me in this reasoning:

Suppose that there is another way to neutralize a criminal. For example, creating their murder weapon, making them think that it is effective, enjoining them to build, on the basis of this effectiveness, their entire plan, so that in the moment that they prepare to shoot, the "weapon" goes back to being what it always was: an illusion.

The entire system, but above all its media, plays the game of creating celebrities whom it later destroys if they don't yield to its designs.

Its power resided (now no longer, as it has been displaced by social media) in deciding what and who existed in the moment when they decided what to name and what to silence.

But really, don't pay much attention to me; as has been evident over these 20 years, I don't know anything about the mass media.

The truth is that this Sup Marcos went from being a spokesperson to being a distraction.

If the path to war, that is to say, the path to death, had taken us 10 years, the path to life required more time and more effort, not to mention more blood.

Because, though you may not believe it, it is easier to die than it is to live.

We needed time to be and to find those who would know how to see us as we are.

We needed time to find those who would see us, not from above or below, but face to face, who would see us with the gaze of a compañero.

So then, as I mentioned, the work of constructing this character began.

One day Marcos' eyes were blue, another day they were green, or brown, or hazel, or black—all depending on who did the interview and took the picture. He was the back-up player of professional soccer teams, an employee in department stores, a chauffeur, philosopher, filmmaker, and the etceteras that can be found in the paid media of those calendars and in various geographies. There was a Marcos for every occasion, that is to say, for every interview. And it wasn't easy, believe me, there was no Wikipedia, and if someone came over from Spain we had to investigate if the Corte Inglés was a typical English-cut suit, a grocery store, or a department store.

If I had to define Marcos the character, I would say without a doubt that he was a mascot suit, a colorful ruse.

We could say, so that you understand me, that Marcos was Non-Free Media (note: this is not the same as being paid media).

In constructing and maintaining this character, we made a few mistakes.

"To err is human," as they say.

During the first year we exhausted, as they say, the repertoire of all possible "Marcoses." And so by the beginning of 1995, we were in a tight spot and the communities' work was only in its initial steps.

And so in 1995 we didn't know what to do. But that was when Zedillo, with the PAN at his side, "discovered" Marcos using the same scientific method used for finding remains, that is to say, by way of an esoteric snitching.

The story of the guy from Tampico gave us some breathing room, even though the subsequent fraud committed by Paca de Lozano made us worry that the paid press would also question the "unmasking" of Marcos and then discover that it was just another fraud. Fortunately, it didn't happen like that. And like this one, the media continued swallowing similar pieces from the rumor mill.

Sometime later, that guy from Tampico showed up here in these lands. Together with Subcomandante Insurgente Moisés, we spoke to him. We offered to do a joint press conference so that he could free himself from persecution, since it would then be obvious that he and Marcos weren't the same person. He didn't want to. He came to live here. He left a few times and his face can be seen in the photographs of the funeral wakes of his parents. You can interview him if you want. Now he lives in a community, in…

[There is a pause here as the speaker leans over to ask Subcomandante Insurgente Moisés if it would be okay to mention where, to which the response is a firm "No."]

Ah, he doesn't want you to know exactly where this man lives. We won't say any more so that if he wants to someday, he can tell the story of what he has lived through since February 9, 1995. On our behalf, we just want to thank him for the information that he has given us which we use from time to time to feed the "certitude" that Sup Marcos is not what he really is, that is to say, a ruse or a hologram, but rather a university professor from that now painful state of Tamaulipas.

In the meantime, we continued looking, looking for you, those of you who are here now and those who are not here but are with us.

We launched various initiatives in order to encounter the other, the other compañero, the other compañera. We tried different initiatives to encounter the gaze and the ear that we need and that we deserve.

In the meantime, our communities continued to move forward, as did the change or hand-off of responsibilities that has been much or little discussed, but which can be confirmed directly, without intermediaries.

In our search of that something else, we failed time and again.

Those who we encountered either wanted to lead us or wanted us to lead them.

There were those who got close to us out of an eagerness to use us, or to gaze backward, be it with anthropological or militant nostalgia.

And so for some we were communists, for others Trotskyists, for others anarchists, for others millenalianists, and I'll leave it there so you can add a few more "-ists" from your own experience.

That was how it was until the "Sixth Declaration of the Lacandon Jungle," the most daring and most Zapatista of all of the initiatives that we have launched up until now.

With the Sixth, we have at last encountered those who can see us face to face and greet us and embrace us, and this is how greetings and embraces are done.

With the Sixth, at last, we found you.

At last, someone who understood that we were not looking for shepherds to guide us, nor flocks to lead to the promised land. Neither masters nor slaves. Neither leaders nor leaderless masses.

But we still didn't know if you would be able to see and hear what we are and what we are becoming.

Internally, the advance of our peoples has been impressive.

And so the course, "Freedom According to the Zapatistas" came about.

Over the three rounds of the course, we realized that there was already a generation that could look at us face to face, that could listen to us and talk to us without seeking a guide or a leader, without intending to be submissive or become followers.

Marcos, the character, was no longer necessary.

The new phase of the Zapatista struggle was ready.

So then what happened, happened, and many of you, compañeros and compañeras of the Sixth, know this firsthand.

They may later say that this thing with the character [of Marcos] was pointless. But an honest look back at those days will show how many people turned to look at us, with pleasure or displeasure, because of the disguises of a colorful ruse, of a mascot.

So you see, the change or handoff of responsibilities is not because of illness or death, nor because of an internal dispute, ouster, or purging.

It comes about logically in accordance with the internal changes that the EZLN has had and is having.

I know this doesn't square with the very square perspectives of those in the various "aboves," but that really doesn't worry us.

And if this ruins the rather poor and lazy explanations of the rumorologoists and zapatologists of Jovel [San Cristobal de las Casas, Chiapas], then oh well.

I am not nor have I been sick, and I am not nor have I been dead.

Or rather, despite the fact that I have been killed so many times, that I have died so many times, here I am again.

And if we ourselves encouraged these rumors, it was because it suited us to do so.

The last great trick of the hologram was to simulate terminal illness, including of the deaths supposedly suffered.

Indeed, the comment "if his health permits" made by Subcomandante Insurgente Moisés in the communiqué announcing the events with the CNI [National Indigenous Congress], was the equivalent of the "if the people ask for me," or "if the polls favor me," or "if it is god's will," and other clichés that have been the crutch of the political class in recent times.

If you will allow me one piece of advice: you should cultivate a bit of a sense of humor, not only for your own mental and physical health, but because without a sense of humor you're not going to understand Zapatismo. And those don't understand, judge; and those who judge, condemn.

In reality, this has been the simplest part of the character. In order to feed the rumor mill it was only necessary to tell a few particular people: "I'm going to tell you a secret but promise me you won't tell anyone."

And of course they told.

The first involuntary collaborators in the rumor about sickness and death have been the "experts in zapatology" in arrogant Jovel and chaotic Mexico City who presume their closeness to and deep knowledge of Zapatismo. In addition to, of course, the police that earn their salaries as journalists, the journalists that earn their salaries as police, and the journalists who only earn salaries, bad ones, as journalists.

Thank you to all of them. Thank you for your discretion. You did exactly what we thought you would do. The only downside of all this is that I doubt anyone will ever tell any of you a secret again.

It is our conviction and our practice that in order to rebel and to struggle, neither leaders nor bosses nor messiahs nor saviors are necessary. To struggle, one only needs a sense of shame, a bit of dignity, and a lot of organization.

As for the rest, it either serves the collective or it doesn't.

What this cult of the individual has provoked in the political experts and analysts "above" has been particularly comical. Yesterday they said that the future of the Mexican people depended on the alliance of two people. The day before yesterday they said that Peña Nieto had become independent of Salinas de Gortari, without realizing that, in this schema, if one criticized Peña Nieto, they were effectively putting themselves on Salinas de Gortari's side, and if one criticized Salinas de Gortari, they were supporting Peña Nieto. Now they say that one has to take sides in the struggle going on "above" over control of telecommunications; in effect, either you're with Slim or you're with Azcárraga-Salinas. And even further above, you're either with Obama or you're with Putin.

Those who look toward, and long to be "above," can continue to seek their leader; they can continue to think that now, for real, the electoral results will be honored; that now, for real, Slim will support the electoral left; that now, for real, the dragons and the battles will appear in *Game of Thrones*; that now, for real, Kirkman will be true to the original comic in the television series *The Walking Dead*; that now, for real, tools made in China aren't going to break on their first use; that now, for real, soccer is going to be a sport and not a business.

And yes, perhaps in some of these cases they will be right. But one can't forget that in all of these cases they are mere spectators, that is, passive consumers.

Those who loved and hated Sup Marcos now know that they have loved and hated a hologram. Their love and hate have been useless, sterile, hollow, empty.

There will not be, then, museums or metal plaques where I was born and raised. There will not be someone who lives off of having been Subcomandante Marcos. No one will inherit his name or his job. There will not be all-paid trips abroad to give lectures. There will not be transport to or care in fancy hospitals. There will not be widows or heirs. There will not be funerals, honors, statues, museums, prizes, or anything else that the system does to promote the cult of the individual and devalue the collective.

This figure was created and now its creators, the Zapatistas, are destroying it.

If anyone understands this lesson from our compañeros and compañeras, they will have understood one of the foundations of Zapatismo.

So, in the last few years, what has happened has happened.

And we saw that now, the outfit, the character, the hologram, was no longer necessary.

Time and time again we planned this, and time and time again we waited for the right moment—the right calendar and geography to show what we really are to those who truly are.

And then Galeano arrived with his death to mark our calendar and geography: "here, in La Realidad (Reality); now; in the pain and rage."

V. PAIN AND RAGE. SIGNS AND SCREAMS.

When we got here to the *caracol* of La Realidad (Reality), without anyone telling us to, we began to speak in whispers.

Our pain spoke quietly, our rage in whispers.

It was as if we were trying to avoid scaring Galeano away with these unfamiliar sounds.

As if our voices and step called to him.

"Wait, *compa*," our silence said.

"Don't go," our words murmured.

But there are other pains and other rages.

At this very minute, in other corners of Mexico and the world, a man, a woman, an other, a little girl, a little boy, an elderly man, an elderly woman, a memory, is beaten cruelly and with impunity, surrounded by the voracious crime that is the system, clubbed, cut, shot, finished off, dragged away among jeers, abandoned, their body then collected and mourned, their life buried.

Just a few names:

Alexis Benhumea, murdered in the State of Mexico.
Francisco Javier Cortés, murdered in the State of Mexico.
Juan Vázquez Guzmán, murdered in Chiapas.
Juan Carlos Gómez Silvano, murdered in Chiapas.
El compa Kuy, murdered in Mexico City.
Carlo Giuliani, murdered in Italy.
Alexis Grigoropoulos, murdered in Greece.
Wajih Wajdi al-Ramahi, murdered in a Refugee Camp in the West Bank city of Ramallah. At age 14, he was shot in the back from an Israeli observation post. There were no marches, protests, or anything else in the streets.
Matías Valentín Catrileo Quezada, Mapuche murdered in Chile.
Teodulfo Torres Soriano, compa of the Sixth, disappeared in Mexico City.
Guadalupe Jerónimo and Urbano Macías, comuneros from Cherán, murdered in Michoacan.
Francisco de Asís Manuel, disappeared in Santa María Ostula.
Javier Martínes Robles, disappeared in Santa María Ostula.
Gerardo Vera Orcino, disappeared in Santa María Ostula.
Enrique Domínguez Macías, disappeared in Santa María Ostula.
Martín Santos Luna, disappeared in Santa María Ostula.
Pedro Leyva Domínguez, murdered in Santa María Ostula.
Diego Ramírez Domínguez, murdered in Santa María Ostula.
Trinidad de la Cruz Crisóstomo, murdered in Santa María Ostula.
Crisóforo Sánchez Reyes, murdered in Santa María Ostula.
Teódulo Santos Girón, disappeared in Santa María Ostula.

Longino Vicente Morales, disappeared in Guerrero.

Víctor Ayala Tapia, disappeared in Guerrero.

Jacinto López Díaz "El Jazi", murdered in Puebla.

Bernardo Vázquez Sánchez, murdered in Oaxaca.

Jorge Alexis Herrera, murdered in Guerrero.

Gabriel Echeverría, murdered in Guerrero.

Edmundo Reyes Amaya, disappeared in Oaxaca.

Gabriel Alberto Cruz Sánchez, disappeared in Oaxaca.

Juan Francisco Sicilia Ortega, murdered in Morelos.

Ernesto Méndez Salinas, murdered in Morelos.

Alejandro Chao Barona, murdered in Morelos.

Sara Robledo, murdered in Morelos.

Juventina Villa Mojica, murdered in Guerrero.

Reynaldo Santana Villa, murdered in Guerrero.

Catarino Torres Pereda, murdered in Oaxaca.

Bety Cariño, murdered in Oaxaca.

Jyri Jaakkola, murdered in Oaxaca.

Sandra Luz Hernández, murdered in Sinaloa.

Marisela Escobedo Ortíz, murdered in Chihuahua.

Celedonio Monroy Prudencio, disappeared in Jalisco.

Nepomuceno Moreno Nuñez, murdered in Sonora.

The migrants, men and women, forcefully disappeared and probably murdered in every corner of Mexican territory.

The prisoners that they want to kill through "life": Mumia Abu Jamal, Leonard Peltier, the Mapuche, Mario González, Juan Carlos Flores.

The continuous burial of voices that were lives, silenced by the sound of the earth thrown over them or the bars closing around them.

And the greatest mockery of all is that with every shovelful of dirt thrown by the thug currently on shift, the system is saying: "You don't count, you are not worth anything, no one will cry for you, no one will be enraged by your death, no one will follow your step, no one will hold up your life."

And with the last shovelful it gives its sentence: "even if they catch and punish those who killed you, we will always find another, an other, to ambush and on whom to repeat the macabre dance that ended your life."

It says: "The small, stunted justice you will be given, manufactured by the paid media to simulate and obtain a bit of calm in order to stop the chaos coming at them, does not scare me, harm me, or punish me."

What do we say to this cadaver who, in whatever corner of the world below, is buried in oblivion?

That only our pain and rage count?

That only our outrage means anything?

That as we murmur our history, we don't hear their cry, their scream?

Injustice has so many names, and provokes so many screams.

But our pain and our rage do not keep us from hearing them.

And our murmurs are not only to lament the unjust fall of our own dead.

They allow us to hear other pains, to make other rages ours, and to continue in the long, complicated, tortuous path of making all of this into a battle cry that is transformed into a freedom struggle.

And to not forget that while someone murmurs, someone else screams.

And only the attentive ear can hear it.

While we are talking and listening right now, someone screams in pain, in rage.

And so it is as if one must learn to direct their gaze; what one hears must find a fertile path.

Because while someone rests, someone else continues the uphill climb.

In order to see this effort, it is enough to lower one's gaze and lift one's heart.

Can you?

Will you be able to?

Small justice looks so much like revenge. Small justice is what distributes impunity; as it punishes one, it absolves others.

What we want, what we fight for, does not end with finding Galeano's murderers and seeing that they receive their punishment (make no mistake, this is what will happen).

The patient and obstinate search seeks truth, not the relief of resignation.

True justice has to do with the buried compañero Galeano.

Because we ask ourselves not what do we do with his death, but what do we do with his life.

Forgive me if I enter into the swampy terrain of commonplace sayings, but this compañero did not deserve to die, not like this.

His tenacity, his daily punctual sacrifice, invisible for anyone other than us, was for life.

And I can assure you that he was an extraordinary being and that, what's more—and this is what amazes—there are thousands of compañeros and compañeras like him in the indigenous Zapatista communities, with the same determination, the same commitment, the same clarity, and one single destination: freedom.

And, doing macabre calculations: if someone deserves death, it is he who does not exist and has never existed, except in the fleeting interest of the paid media.

As our compañero, chief and spokesperson of the EZLN, Subcomandante Insurgente Moisés has already told us, in killing Galeano, or any Zapatista, those above are trying to kill the EZLN.

Not the EZLN as an army, but as the rebellious and stubborn force that builds and raises life where those above desire the wasteland brought by the mining, oil, and tourist industries, the death of the earth and those who work and inhabit it.

He has also said that we have come, as the General Command of the Zapatista Army for National Liberation, to exhume Galeano.

We think that it is necessary for one of us to die so that Galeano lives.

To satisfy the impertinence that is death, in place of Galeano we put another name, so that Galeano lives and death takes not a life but just a name—a few letters empty of any meaning, without their own history or life.

That is why we have decided that Marcos today will cease to exist.

He will go hand-in-hand with Shadow the Warrior and the Little Light so that he doesn't get lost on the way. Don Durito will go with him, Old Man Antonio also.

The little girls and boys who used to crowd around to hear his stories will not miss him; they are grown up now, they have their own capacity for discernment; they now struggle like him for freedom, democracy, and justice, which is the task of every Zapatista.

It is the cat-dog, and not a swan, who will sing his farewell song.

And in the end, those who have understood will know that he who never was here does not leave; that he who never lived does not die.

And death will go away, fooled by an indigenous man whose *nom de guerre* was Galeano, and those rocks that have been placed on his tomb will once again walk and teach whoever will listen the most basic tenet of Zapatismo, that is: don't sell out, don't give in, don't give up.

Oh death! As if it wasn't obvious that it frees those above of any responsibility beyond the funeral prayer, the bland homage, the sterile statue, the controlling museum.

And for us? Well, for us death commits us to the life it contains.

So here we are, mocking death in Reality (La Realidad).

Compas:

Given the above, at 2:08 am on May 25, 2014, from the southeast combat front of the EZLN, I here declare that he who is known as Subcomandante Insurgente Marcos, self-proclaimed "Subcomandante of Stainless Steel," ceases to exist.

That is how it is.

Through my voice the Zapatista Army for National Liberation no longer speaks.

OK. *Salud* and until never or until forever; those who have understood will know that this doesn't matter anymore, that it never has.

From the Zapatista reality, La Realidad
Subcomandante Insurgente Marcos.

P.S. 1. Game over?

P.S. 2. Check mate?

P.S. 3. Touché?

P.S. 4. Go make sense of it, *raza*, and send tobacco.

P.S. 5. Hmm… so this is hell… It's Piporro, Pedro, José Alfredo! What? For being *machista*? Nah, I don't think so, since I've never…

P.S. 6. Great, now that the mask has come off, I can walk around here naked, right?

P.S.7. Hey, it's really dark here, I need a little light.

(…)

[He lights his pipe and exits stage left. Subcomandante Insurgente Moisés announces that "another compañero is going to say a few words."]

(a voice is heard offstage)

Good morning compañeras and compañeros. My name is Galeano, Subcomandante Insurgente Galeano.

Anyone else here named Galeano?

[the crowd cries, "We are all Galeano!"]

Ah, that's why they told me that when I was reborn, it would be as a collective.

And so it should be.

Have a good journey. Take care of yourselves, take care of us.

From the mountains of the Mexican Southeast,
Subcomandante Insurgente Galeano.

THE SKI MASK AS PREFACE (OR PREFACE WITH A SKI
MASK)
Gabriela Juaregui

You have been reading the writings of a hologram. The texts of someone who no longer exists, or perhaps never really existed. Subcomandante Insurgente Marcos died over three years ago in May, 2014 to give life to Subcomandante Insurgente Galeano. The writings of a dead man living—a contradiction embodied. So why a hologram then? Because, as any holographic image, this persona or character (or both) is 'a multiplicity in unity,' indivisible except intensively, as Henry Bortoft explains in *Taking Appearance Seriously*, as the hologram remains whole even when divided. This voice is a whole, made up of several other voices. A voice that is never/always one.

What you have read, therefore, are the texts of a hologram as translator. As Marcos himself explained in an interview with Jorge Ramos, "Marcos is the name of a *compañero* who died, and we always took the names of those who died, with the idea that one never dies but keeps fighting on." The name is a translation, moving from one person to another, and so Marcos' identity, his very tongue, is another. The name is a mask, and the mask is not a mask, as the Zapatistas all explain, but rather the face, "the face that had to be covered in order to be seen," so as to pierce the blindness of racism. Mono-meanings happily destabilized and fixed id-entities too. Many people started chanting in support of the Zapatistas soon after their uprising, "We are all Marcos," and in a way, so are you, if you listen, if you let these words not just into your minds, but into your hearts and bodies. The voice living in these texts is not that of the singular character behind the famous ski mask; rather what lives and breathes in these texts is the rebel imagination of the Indigenous communities of Chiapas. And in order for us to understand this imagination, here is Marcos, the translator. His is a tongue that cracks open silence, but in a language people outside the communities might be able to hear and understand, and perhaps, finally, listen to.

Marcos is therefore triply translating as he both moves [information] from one place to another, from one specific geography to many others, and moves us as readers; but, also, as one traditionally understands it, he is translating from one language or worldview into another, from one culture to another, so that we may begin to understand that very rebel imagination. And it's not that this imagination did not exist before these texts. It's nothing new. What is new is that we can now listen and understand it. Marcos's translation labor, even his belaboring, is to our benefit. And perhaps this is why in 1994, suddenly, and despite the mass media and government's efforts to label them as terrorists, the Zapatistas gained national and international sympathy so that a few days after their insurgency, on January 8th 1994, there was a massive march asking for peace. Marcos' performance as translator worked.

To understand this tremendous task, it is essential to imagine, to know, to embody this knowledge in our flesh: until 1994, the *caxlanes* and *coletos* or white and mestizo inhabitants of San Cristobal de las Casas, Chiapas, did not allow indigenous people to even *walk* on the sidewalk; they would force them down to the street. The indigenous communities of the region did not exist, as they were made invisible and oppressed by ongoing colonial practices, by the very project of Modernity itself. And then on January 1st 1994, Marcos declares: "We apologize for the inconvenience. This is a revolution." We apologize, sir, but we *will* walk on the same sidewalk. We apologize, ma'am, but we are human; we are Mexican just as you are, says the Revolution. We apologize if this derails your vacation plans, dear foreign tourist. We have rights. We demand freedom and justice. From day one there is Marcos, behind his ski mask, pipe in hand, translating, speaking in name of this collective—as he says in various texts "through my voice speaks the voice of…"— and from day one, in the middle of an uprising, there is even humor in his translations.

From day one, this voice is a multiplicity: "The echo that takes its place and speaks its own voice and speaks the voice of the other. / The echo that reproduces its own sound and opens itself to the sound of the other. / The echo of this rebel voice transforming itself and renewing itself in other voices," as he writes in the "Second Declaration of La Realidad for Humanity and Against Neoliberalism." An echo—multiplicity in unity.

In his letter in reply to John Berger, who mentioned that writing is the approximation of experience, Marcos ponders whether it is not also an act of distancing. The self-conscious translator complicates his own position. "And I imagine, Mr. Berger, that the final result of the relationship between the writer and the reader, through the text ('or from the image,' insists my other self again), escapes both." And opens up an enigma. Hence the artfulness of these texts as well. Marcos the writer, the translator, the persona, the character, uses all kinds of literary forms and genres, he often talks to himself, and is variously interrupted while also in humorous almost allegorical dialogue with a series of recurring comrades/characters (el Viejo Antonio being perhaps the most important of all) whereby he becomes a sort of narrator of a bildungsroman, in the quest of learning, in the process of becoming other. In this way, holo-grammatically and in a multiplicity of selves that dialogue with each other, he is also the stand-in for us readers in the process of learning how to listen. He is also a trickster figure, whose last authored text states, "if you allow me to define Marcos the character, I would say without hesitation he was a mascot suit. Let's say, so that you may understand me, that Marcos was an unfree medium/media (note that it's different from being a paid media/medium[1])." Always humorous and self-deprecating, using his false naiveté to teach a lesson, and his modesty to remind us he, Marcos, is not what matters here, even if his name is on the cover of the

---

1   From "Between Light and Shadow". Note that *medio* in Spanish can both allude to a medium or the media and as is customary with Marcos's word play, he is probably toying with both meanings. The mascot suit in the Spanish is *botarga*, which refers to those larger-than-life cartoonlike suits.

book or if he did end up becoming an icon, his writing style mimicked and echoed by so many of us throughout our youth.

Although part of this translator's biography has come to light, it is nevertheless irrelevant. What the EZLN does let us know is that this translator had been there many years prior and that this white or mestizo man is not really the one speaking. He could not speak as a white man; the white man had already been defeated. Marcos tells of how there were six of them who went into the jungle in the '80s and how their first military defeat was inflicted upon them by the indigenous communities there. If Marcos died to give life to Galeano, before that, the one who is behind the ski mask was also already dead to give life to Marcos, and in all likelihood his death was more catastrophic. But all these biographical references are absurd and anecdotal. Who cares? Whoever died to give life to Marcos, who dies in turn to give life to Galeano, died to give life to a collective voice. This is the voice of the texts in this book.

The collective voice contained in these texts is full of symbols and metaphors that reveal a mastery of performance and symbol manipulation. Marcos often uses the symbols of nationalism to turn them on their head and reveal that if the communities of Chiapas are not considered truly Mexican, then nothing is. This voice is also a masterful use of the internet in its early days as well as a calculated use of certain media. Marcos's use of symbols also reveals our own racism, since we focused on Marcos the icon; while he never was the real heart of the movement, he was its instrument in the best possible sense. Marcos, in his own words, "went from being a spokesperson to being a distraction." (From *Between Light and Shadow*) The hologram translator is necessary as communities were well aware of this pervasive racism. It is partly against it that they rebel, and they were also quite conscious of the racism lurking behind even the friendliest and most committed rebel consciences. For instance, when in 2001, after Vicente Fox is elected, there is a countrywide march called "The Color of the Earth," in which various indigenous leaders and the Sup, as he is known affectionately, hit the road to discuss the San Andrés agreements. During the tour they took turns speaking, sometimes one or another, but when Marcos would come onstage, people clamored "Marcos! Marcos!" making it clear that sometimes even this translator was misunderstood as being something else—more celebrity than collective. People had turned him into a rock star, effectively killing him, therefore intensifying the invisibility of the other indigenous comandantas and comandantes. Whereas el Sup would have liked to disappear, to blend in with the rest of the ski masks, we were the ones who would not allow him to evaporate and gave substance to the hologram, projecting our own misunderstandings and suppressed racism. And that's why Marcos had to die also, and again.

This is his voice that is not one, his tongue that is another and another and another, the many-petaled "flower for this tender fury—I think it deserves one." Still.

OTHER TITLES FROM THE SONG CAVE

1. *A Dark Dreambox of Another Kind* by **Alfred Starr Hamilton**
2. *My Enemies* by **Jane Gregory**
3. *Rude Woods* by **Nate Klug**
4. *Georges Braque and Others* by **Trevor Winkfield**
5. *The Living Method* by **Sara Nicholson**
6. *Splash State* by **Todd Colby**
7. *Essay Stanzas* by **Thomas Meyer**
8. *Illustrated Games of Patience* by **Ben Estes**
9. *Dark Green* by **Emily Hunt**
10. *Honest James* by **Christian Schlegel**
11. *M* by **Hannah Brooks-Motl**
12. *What the Lyric Is* by **Sara Nicholson**
13. *The Hermit* by **Lucy Ives**
14. *The Orchid Stories* by **Kenward Elmslie**
15. *Do Not Be a Gentleman When You Say Goodnight* by **Mitch Sisskind**
16. *HAIRDO* by **Rachel B. Glaser**
17. *Motor Maids across the Continent* by **Ron Padgett**
18. *Songs for Schizoid Siblings* by **Lionel Ziprin**